Anatomy of
an Undeclared War

Congressional Conference

on the Pentagon Papers

Foreword by Ernest Gruening

Edited by Patricia A. Krause

INTERNATIONAL UNIVERSITIES PRESS, INC.

NEW YORK

Library of Congress Catalog Card Number: 72–80552

ISBN: 0–8236–0147–1

43455

This book is dedicated to a swift return to the open democratic society envisioned by our founding fathers, one with three coequal branches of government, an aggressive press, and a well-informed electorate.

Contents

EDITOR'S PREFACE   9
FOREWORD—ERNEST GRUENING   11
STATEMENT OF PURPOSE   17
Chapter 1. CULPABILITY AND RESPONSIBILITY   21
Chapter 2. THE WAR IS GRINDING ON   73
Chapter 3. "THE SOUTHERN DUCK WANTS TO LIE DOWN"   89
Chapter 4. U.S. FOREIGN POLICY APPRAISAL:
     IMPLICATIONS FOR THE FUTURE   135
Photographs of Participants   171
Profiles of Contributors to the Congressional
     Conference on the Pentagon Papers   177
APPENDIX 1. Congress' Interest in *The New York
     Times* and *The Washington Post* Cases   199
APPENDIX 2. A Right to Know as Well as a Right to
     Publish—*The Washington Post*   212
APPENDIX 3. Counterbriefing on U.S. Policy in
     Indochina   235

Editor's Preface

When the Pentagon Papers first surfaced in *The New York Times* and *The Washington Post* in June of 1971, the resulting furor over the Justice Department's move to enjoin publication occupied the front pages of most newspapers across the country. At a meeting held in late June, seventeen Members of Congress decided that while the public was aware of the government's attempts to stifle freedom of the press, people generally were not informed about the actual contents of the papers and their significance. These Congressmen therefore concluded that they would hold a three-day conference—open to the public and press—on the Pentagon Papers. Outside experts would be invited to participate in a discussion on the contents of the papers, with a view to further raising the consciousness of the people of this country regarding United States involvement in Indochina.

Nineteen outside participants—rich in a knowledge of Southeast Asia—agreed to attend, and together with the seventeen Congressional sponsors took part in the discussions, July 27 through July 29, in Washington, D.C. Representative John Dow of New York chaired the meetings.

This book contains an edited transcript of the conference proceedings and additional supplementary material related to the subject matter. Former Senator Gruening kindly consented to write the foreword, the sentiment of which is further detailed in a statement of purpose prepared under the direction of the sponsors.

The conference represented the fourth in a series sponsored over the years by basically the same group of Congressmen. The first in January of 1966 was concerned with the escalation of the Vietnam war. The second, on national priorities and military spending, was held in March of 1969, and was published in book form as *American Militarism: 1970* by The Viking Press. And in 1970, the third conference, the Congressional Conference on War and National Responsibility, dealt with the subject of war crimes, which appeared as *War Crimes and the American Conscience*, published in 1970 by Holt, Rinehart and Winston.

The editor gratefully acknowledges the cooperation of the conference participants and the staffs of the congressional sponsors. Additionally, tribute should be paid to Diane James, Paula Katz, Karen Ohmans and Carl Rogers for their efforts on behalf of both the conference and the publication of this book. Thanks are also due to Norma Fox, editor at International Universities Press, for her commitment and application to this project. Finally, special mention must be made of Frank Greer for his invaluable contributions.

PATRICIA A. KRAUSE

Washington, D.C., April 1972

[10]

Foreword

The decision of seventeen Congressmen to publicly air the Pentagon Papers is an auspicious beginning marking a long overdue effort to re-establish the basic principles which our nation has professed for nearly two centuries.

Hopefully the first result of this endeavor will be to inform the public. This in itself is the converse of, and the proper and desirable reaction to, the secrecy which has shrouded the performance of public officials. Under cover of this concealment, deliberately contrived, the perpetration of infamous deeds have been purposefully obscured and kept hidden from the American people. Hence, exposure, repeated exposure, is the first requirement. Following such revelation—which this administration has gone to great lengths to prevent—we must interpret and make clear the enormity of these betrayals. This done we shall need to analyze the causes responsible for such incredible departures from the accepted norms, and having uncovered the motivations and origins, we must strive to prevent their recurrence henceforth.

Let us for a moment turn our attention to what has hap-

pened to us at the hands of a few entrusted with responsibility and power. We have been lied into the costliest, bloodiest, and most indefensible misadventure in our history, the consequences of which although still unfathomable are unmistakably malevolent. No good whatsoever can come of this monstrous war. Among its consequences are some sixty thousand Americans dead and close to half a million wounded; here we find the blinded, armless, legless and paralyzed, not to mention those who have been psychologically injured beyond repair. All have bled and died in vain, all have been wantonly sacrificed in the service of a cause which is worse than worthless. As if this were not gruesome enough, our casualties are multiplied ten-fold or more by those of the Southeast Asians—Vietnamese, Laotians, Cambodians—a million or more of whom have been slaughtered, crippled or reduced to homeless refugees; we have spared neither women nor children nor the aged. We have made a wasteland of three little countries. And what is perhaps most bizarre, their destruction has been wedded to an image of America as a peace-loving, treaty-abiding, trustworthy, civilized nation. This war has brutalized and cynicized vast numbers of us. It has alienated our young people, many of whom have lost faith in our system of government. Unless their faith can be restored our great venture in freedom, begun so brilliantly nearly two centuries ago, is in dire peril.

To salvage our freedom requires preliminarily the information that repeated exposure will provide. From this information there must evolve a resulting determination that the macabre performances revealed by the Pentagon Papers shall not recur. Finally, appropriate action must be taken at the polling places. Ultimately, the deceivers must be thrown out.

It is useless to look for reforms if the same rascals remain in power. Unless they are repudiated, they, or others like

[12]

them, will simply repeat their deceits and their betrayals.

Nearly two centuries ago, a handful of men had a wholly different vision, which was backed by the resolve to initiate a great experiment. Theirs was a radical concept in its day. They postulated that people were *entitled* to life, liberty and the pursuit of happiness—ideas scarcely dreamed of in the old world—and that governments were instruments to procure this objective. This goal was predicated on freedom of speech, of assembly, of the press, of worship, freedom from search and seizure. Their experiment, which has served us so well for nearly two hundred years is much too precious to be allowed to perish. What the Pentagon Papers reveal is sickness at the core, the exposure of which has furnished a key to the search for remedies and their application

It would do us well if, from this nucleus of dedicated citizens, congressmen and others, the truths told by the Pentagon Papers could be made more generally available. They should not only be widely disseminated, but their significance analyzed and summarized for those who have not had the opportunity to digest them to their full extent. It is to our greatest interest to arouse the conscience and mobilize the innate decency of the masses of Americans. These representatives on the Hill have shown the way. Let them and the rest of us who are concerned keep at it. In the inspiring words of one of their colleagues, "Let's make America happen again."

Ernest Gruening
Washington, D.C.

Anatomy of
an Undeclared War

Statement of Purpose

A PRIMARY effect of this conference has been to intensify the sense of outrage we share with many of our fellow Americans over the deceptions, the arrogance of power, and the callous disregard for the Constitution, all of which is clearly documented in the Pentagon Papers.

We have concluded that the responsibility for our disastrous course of action over the past twenty years in Southeast Asia belongs not only to our Presidents, but also to the Congress, to the people and to the press of this nation.

We remain deeply concerned about the present course of the Vietnam war. It is patently clear that we persist in the merciless killing of the Asian people and the destruction of their countries. While the President maintains, on the one hand, that he is "winding down the war" by gradually reducing United States ground forces in Southeast Asia, on the other hand, he increases the bombings in those countries.

Tactics change but the policy endures: senseless death and destruction. The public must realize, and the Congress must accept responsibility for, the fact that "Vietnamization" is only a euphemism for more killing.

[17]

But it is not the war policy alone that endures. As one Conference participant accurately noted, the "greater concern is the pattern of deception in United States foreign policy—deception of the Congress and the American people. The truth about United States objectives in Indochina is being distorted or hidden as much now as before, and this circumstance is as intolerable as the policies themselves."

It is imperative that Congress demand a full report on American bombing in Northern and Southern Laos, Cambodia and Vietnam—on the Phoenix program and the forced relocation of the South Vietnamese—on United States involvement in the South Vietnam elections and on the Administration's failure to respond positively to the latest proposal by the National Liberation Front.*

Congress has failed not only in its duty to exercise a vaguely defined right of oversight; it has been equally remiss in its obligation to challenge critically the foreign-policy assumptions of the Executive branch. This is not simple negativism. Rather, historically, human judgments are best when exposed to relentless cross-examination. When that process fails, the essence of our government—balanced and checked powers—fails. Such deterioration cannot continue indefinitely without gravely jeopardizing the survival and progress of our form of government.

Without this cross-examination, the public's role in foreign policy diminishes. An aggressive Executive branch which proceeds unimpeded by a lethargic Congress cannot be effectively questioned by the people. Resignation and cynicism become the response of an uninformed public. Elections, particularly for the Congress, become contests based on superficial and peripheral issues. As a consequence, the most important ques-

---

* Temporal references must be viewed in terms of events subsequent to this conference.

tions of peace and even survival cannot be meaningfully presented for the vigorous debate they deserve. The result is election and re-election of members of Congress who ultimately reflect the voting behavior of an unenlightened public.

The necessary tension between the press and the government faltered as we settled into the quagmire in Southeast Asia. The hesitancy of significant segments of the press to promote broad public debate on the war must be regarded as a failure of government to govern itself. A heroic press might have significantly altered the course of events in the early 1960's. But perhaps even more important than the need for heroics was the need for ordinary men and women, both in government and outside, to have the opportunity to question policy intelligently.

This Conference arrived at certain preliminary conclusions.

If Congress is to reassert its proper constitutional role in the area of foreign policy, it must develop and use independent sources of information. Congress and the people will never be in a position to make sound judgments if they must rely solely on the Executive branch for their information.

Specifically, we recommend that Congress:

- establish an office of foreign policy analysis to advise Congress and to evaluate our foreign policy in various areas of the world. The office might also award scholarships to train students in the field of foreign policy analysis. Reports of the office to Congress would be made public unless Congress voted to withhold the information.
- implement the Legislative Reorganization Act of 1970 to provide itself with the staff and equipment absolutely essential for coping with the complexities of a $200-billion-a-year government operation.

[19]

  • emphasize the responsibility of the General Accounting Office to initiate periodic reviews of the foreign aid expenditures of the State and Defense Departments.

  • accept the responsibility to question assumptions and applications of our foreign policy. No supply of information can substitute for the present lack of congressional will to assume this responsibility.

Beyond these long-range recommendations, we face the central matter of greatest urgency—the immediate withdrawal of United States forces from Southeast Asia. The responsibility for peace lies not only with the Administration—it lies with the Congress and with the people.

Sponsors

James G. Abourezk	Michael Harrington
Phillip Burton	Henry Helstoski
John Conyers, Jr.	Robert W. Kastenmeier
John G. Dow	Edward I. Koch
Robert Frederick Drinan	Abner J. Mikva
Bob Eckhardt	Parren Mitchell
Don Edwards	Benjamin S. Rosenthal
Donald M. Fraser	William Fitts Ryan

John F. Seiberling

Washington, D. C.
August 4, 1971

CHAPTER ONE

Culpability and Responsibility

<hr>

DR. ELLSBERG: By December of this year, the Congress of the United States will have been appropriating taxpayers' money to spend on, in part to support, a war in Indochina which has been dragging on for twenty-five years—a quarter of a century.

Last May marked the twentieth anniversary of the month in which the Executive initially asked Congress to supply funds for use directly in the war in Indochina, a request with which Congress complied. For each year, then, of these last twenty years, money has been appropriated by Congress for napalm, for hiring Vietnamese soldiers (initially to fight against their own independence) and for planes and other equipment in that war.

This means that a young man who was born in the month of May, 1950, would now be able to vote on these issues, even prior to the new voting regulations which reduce the voting age.

But for each year of his life, his parents would have paid taxes, voted by the Congress, to support that war, and for each of the last three years, he would have faced a serious

possibility of being drafted for service in that war, something which no Frenchman in the eight years of the French war, supported by us against the independence of Vietnam, ever had to face.

One Vietnamese who objected strongly during that first Indochina war to the use of United States-produced and -supplied napalm against his countrymen who were fighting for their independence, was a patriot and a nationalist named Ngo Dinh Diem.

Later, thanks to us, he became the ruler and eventually the dictator of South Vietnam. In that role he asked for American napalm to be used against his countrymen. He got it. He also, for the first time, asked the United States to supply defoliants and herbicides, and Congress voted the money for that as well.

The taxpayers and Congress giveth. The Executive giveth and the Executive taketh away. When it came time to discard Ngo Dinh Diem, the signal given to the plotters in Vietnam of United States support for the coup in 1963 was that the Executive should suspend payment on the Commodity Import Program which supported their entire military budget: again, these were funds that had always been supplied by Congress.

When the Executive did so in the fall of 1963, as the Pentagon Papers show, the coup plotters then benefited from the realization on the part of every officer in the Vietnamese army that he faced a total loss of United States support for the military budget. That is, the officers' salaries and pay for their troops would be cut off unless they joined the coup opposing Diem. Needless to say, they complied. Diem was assassinated. This act of liberation of the Vietnamese people that we had supported for so long was so popular that Minh, the man who led that coup, is today widely recognized as the most popular and respected figure in the Vietnamese armed forces.

He is a man so politically significant that he could run

against the incumbent president, who benefits from all the advantages of United States support now, and would, in fact, be a sure winner this year in the campaign were it not for the fact that it is against United States policy that he win. So his chances for winning are, in fact, minimal. [1]

One more anniversary—one that's almost the first. Last December, Congress was asked to vote upon a supplemental appropriation that would extend and support the use of American firepower in Cambodia as well as Laos.

It is obvious that firepower is not for the benefit of the people of Laos. What it has done for the people of Cambodia— where the population is a little under seven million—is create a million refugees since the time of our invasion with the South Vietnamese in 1970. [2]

Two senators voted against that supplemental appropriation —Gore and Goodell—both lame ducks in part because they had incurred the hostility of the administration for their acts of opposition to the war. But that number constitutes the proportion of Congressmen that had always opposed appropriation bills year after year.

We are honored here by the presence of one of the two Senators—Senator Gruening—who voted against the Tonkin Gulf resolution, voted against its hasty passage, and as we now can see from the Pentagon Papers, its deceptively manipulated passage at that time.

Now the kind of history that I have just presented is couched in language that would have been regarded only three months ago as emotional, biased, fanatic, extreme. I know this because I have been called all of these things whenever I sug-

---

[1] Minh later dropped out of the running, charging collusion between the United States and Thieu.

[2] According to the Kennedy Subcommittee on Refugees, there are currently about two million refugees.

gested anything approaching this over the last couple of years, that is, since I first read the Pentagon Papers.

There are still columnists and politicians who will use these terms to describe our Congressional involvement and what it has meant. But when I hear such interpretations I generally assume that they are from someone who has not yet read the Pentagon Papers.

I know how hard it is to get anyone to read the Pentagon Papers. No one knows better than I. They are singularly tedious. They are unquestionably boring. They are stultifying. Nonetheless, I happen to think there is no substitute for reading very substantial portions of those papers, unfortunately even more than is available at present. A book has been published, thanks to *The New York Times* and Bantam Books, which does give the general public and Congressmen, and for that matter, uninformed people in the Pentagon, a chance to become much better informed than previously. I would hope that the Congressmen will undertake to ensure, and they have the power to do this, that the entire record is available—not a selected part, not a small bit, but the entire seven thousand pages, which for all its limitations is a massive beginning on the honest history of the war. [3]

I think that measures which would make this information available to Congressional staff as well as to the Congressmen themselves and ultimately to the public should be heartily encouraged. Nevertheless, this history does show very clearly that the Executive is on fairly firm ground when it claims that it has had the supporting collaboration of Congress in waging this war over the last twenty years.

[3] Subsequent to this, two other editions of the Pentagon Papers were published: *United States–Vietnam Relations, 1945–1967*, Washington, D.C.: Government Printing Office, 1971; and *The Senator Gravel Edition—The Pentagon Papers*, Boston: Beacon Press, 1971. Neither includes the four volumes on negotiations which are in the hands of Congressional committees.

Many Congressmen have honorably spoken out strongly and truly about the war, but so long as they themselves—and this is true of most of them—vote for the appropriations, they have given the President all that he requires of them to help wage the war.

In short, they have given him their collaboration and their cooperation, and thus they are accomplices in the war, as each President has pointed out.

On the other hand, the responsibility of those who have been lied to is not the same. It is not so great as the responsibility of those doing the lying. Even among those who have been deceived, who range in some degree from citizens to the President, the responsibilities are not the same.

Among those lied to, there are differences of degree of responsibility corresponding to their varying powers to have known or found out the truth. One question to be asked, for example, is whether Congressmen have used to the full their Constitutional powers to seek out, and inform themselves of, the truth.

From now on, thanks to the Pentagon Papers, any Congressman who remains ignorant of the data and information in those studies takes upon himself a very heavy individual responsibility for his own ignorance and his own decisions that may follow from it.

The same holds true for the administration, of course, for each day that it persists in denying this information to the United States public. But supposing this responsibility—to inform themselves—is faced as it has not been in the past. What can anyone do about it? Specifically, what can a Congressman do about it? He knows the details of what is open to him far better than I.

But I do want to suggest a standard by which congressional efforts can be judged. Weighing heavily on the members of

[25]

Congress this year, as in the past, is the fact that if they use their power to end the war, they can end it.

The inhibition against using that power has been that the President, as he has made clear, will not share that responsibility with Congress. To me, the meaning of the support for the McGovern-Hatfield amendment and others, such as it has been, is that many Congressmen are willing to share that responsibility for helping the President to get out of Vietnam.

But, as I say, the President has made it clear that Congress will have to fight him, to get us out. That is, Congress will have to take all the responsibility. Senator Stennis articulated what was on the minds of many Congressmen. He warned his colleagues against a bill that would give Congress sole responsibility for ending the war by ending appropriations. Thus, the responsibility for any bad consequences that might follow would rest with Congress.

God knows there is no guarantee that only good consequences will follow from that act either in this country or in Vietnam. So Stennis urged his fellow Congressmen not to take upon themselves the recriminations that would follow from that responsibility.

While this is humanly understandable, it is also true that to dodge such responsibility is to accept the responsibility for continuing the war. A Congressman's willingness to fight the President on this matter would be shown by his efforts to cut off appropriations; to move where appropriate in terms of violations of international law and the Constitution toward impeachment of various officials who may be found unequivocally to have lied or to have misused their Constitutional power; or to file suits against these officials, as I am glad to see some Congressmen have done; to obstruct Executive-desired legislation, appropriations, or appointments, not only by adverse votes but by such means as filibuster if necessary,

to obtain Executive compliance; and to support legislation which would reassert the constitutional role of Congress—the making of foreign policy and its war powers.

To do such things, a Congressman must be willing to risk the loss of votes; he must be willing to risk the loss of financial support and a sympathetic press. He will certainly lose points within the club, as Senator Gravel did when he tried to inform the people of the contents of the Papers.

He will be publicly embarrassed. He will be criticized and laughed at. Nothing is more ominous to a politician, I think. He may lose his job. Is it reasonable to ask him to take those risks in this case?

I think the standard that each individual, and specifically Congressmen, should take in judging whether he personally has done enough is set by two types of behavior that are familiar to all of us.

The first is the standard of the three million men who have answered the call of Congress and the Executive and risked their bodies and their lives in the paddies, jungles and cities of South Vietnam.

How many of them have paid for that willingness with their arms and their legs? That is a statistic, I understand, Congress has not yet been able to pry out of the Department of Defense, which apparently believes the American public has no need to know how many of its sons have suffered such losses.

But we do know that fifty-five thousand have given their lives while hundreds are spending time in foreign prisons because they felt it was their responsibility to answer the demands of Congress and the President.

Second, there are several hundred prisoners of war in this country—young men, who before they had ever heard of the Pentagon Papers, instinctively knew it was not right for them to go to war; that, in fact, it was their duty as Americans, as

free, responsible human beings, not to collaborate but to resist that war; and they are in prison for this decision today, while thousands of others are in jeopardy for such resistance.

At least one of these young men, Vincent McGee, is known to many of the Congressional sponsors of this conference. Mr. McGee devoted his last months, while the Supreme Court was considering his case for draft resistance, to Business Executives' Move for Peace, working on the Hill to inform Congressmen and encourage them to resist the war. That is how they know him.

He was married while waiting for the Supreme Court decision a couple of months ago. He is now an inmate at Lewisburg Prison on counts that include not having a draft card.

Vincent McGee took half of his draft card and burned it in April of 1967, he sent the other half to Lyndon Johnson. I asked him a month ago, while he was waiting to go to prison, why he had chosen that form of activity rather than simply using the electoral process; why he had dramatically chosen to expose himself to prison in order to express his deep moral conscientious feelings against the war.

He told me something very interesting. I asked him how old he was in 1967. He was twenty-four years old. I said, "That means you were twenty-one in 1964." He said, "Yes, that was the first year I voted. I voted for Lyndon Johnson as a candidate who would get us out of this war and would be for peace."

"The only President that 1 have ever known, that I have ever voted for, is the man who told me that, and by 1967 it was clear to me that voting alone was not all that I could do nor all that I must do to end this war."

Nor is it all that those Congressmen who know Vinnie McGee can do either. I think the answer to the question of what is one's responsibility and how ingenious and resolute

one should be in opposing the war is contingent on the following:

What could you do to resist the war, if you were willing to risk the loss of your job or your career, your influence on or access to powerful people?

No one here will be asked to give his life in opposing the war, as your brothers and sons have been asked or perhaps will be asked.

That is not the issue for you. It is not the issue for me or for anyone here. But there are people here who have relatives or friends who have chosen to go to jail in opposing the war. When it comes to lesser indignities, such as the embarrassment Senator Gravel experienced, I know that he felt it was well worth the effort. I know he would have been willing to endure even greater discomfort in the service of the truth.

Hence, I am speaking here in a real feeling of hope that Congressmen, like other citizens, when they have the information on which to make a responsible choice, will do so and will use their power to end this war.

REP. ECKHARDT: I think a basic failing in our system is that we have not devised a means by which Congress can be sufficiently advised of certain matters about which it should have knowledge.

I am not only talking about events of the past. For instance, we are presently considering the question of setting off a nuclear device with a five-megaton magnitude in the Aleutians.

It is my understanding that there are some seven papers advising the President with respect to whether this is desirable. It is also my understanding that they advise that it is *not* desirable; yet the Congress can not obtain this information even at this late date. Congresswoman Mink has been asking many different sources for this information between the time

of authorization and the time of appropriations on this subject. It is extremely important for Congress to know what the technical advice is with respect to this matter.

It seems to me that the Pentagon Papers point up a severe flaw in the system: that is, the matter of excessive classification, and the failure to make available that type of information which is absolutely necessary for intelligent policy decision making on the part of the Congress.

REP. MIKVA: I would like to ask Mr. Chomsky whether there were any relevant times when Congress could have intervened, given our present institutions and our present policy? Or do we have to work out a whole new oversight procedure to avoid mistakes in the future that we have made in the past?

DR. CHOMSKY: I think Congress could have intervened in the beginning, when United States involvement began, around 1950, when we began financing the French effort to recover their former colony. And from that step on, at each and every step, whether it was the early violation of the Geneva Agreement by sending 300 men in addition to those permitted, or whether it was money appropriated, there was Congressional participation. There was certainly opportunity for investigation, but the Congress at every point failed to accept its responsibility under our constitutional system, exactly as the President and his advisors refused to accept their obligations under valid treaties, such as the United Nations Charter, which prohibits the threat or use of force in international affairs. So, at least as far as this event goes, it is not the "system" in a narrow sense that is wrong but rather the absolute failure to make use of it.

REP. EDWARDS: Five administrations have followed the same

course, and I think most of us knew an awful lot about what was going on, but not as explicitly as is the case now when we see it all written down. To see what was going on in 1961, 1962 and 1963 is almost unbelievable.

And Congress did nothing—zero—to the committees charged with oversight that could have exercised their oversight because, I think, Congress approved of what was going on. All of the administrations have stated over and over again in the Pentagon Papers that this war must be won, that there must be a non-Communist government in South Vietnam.

I think a great many members of the Congress do what they think is right, even though we might disagree with what they think is right. But certainly they have been supporting the war with all of these billions and billions of dollars, and the consequences thereof, because they thought that the Pentagon and the White House were doing something they believed to be proper.

REP. DOW: You probably recall at the time we began the bombing of North Vietnam in 1965 that the State Department put out a paper called "Aggression in the North," and in that paper there was considerable documentation of aggression by North Vietnamese in South Vietnam.

To be sure, some of the aggressors were born in South Vietnam, but nevertheless, the point was made that there was aggression from North Vietnam.

Now, in reading the Pentagon Papers I have been somewhat surprised to learn a good deal more about the activities running in the other direction, that is, from our side, directed at North Vietnam, and admittedly so.

The Papers not only speak of cold-blooded operations, but they detail operations opposing North Vietnam by sending bodies of South Vietnamese to North Vietnam as early as

1954. They also refer to one type of operation named 34-A which seemed to be operations inside North Vietnam. Finally, there was the Desoto Operation which was apparently a naval operation off the east coast of North Vietnam.

Now, these events clearly demonstrate that there was action running from our side against North Vietnam, which came as quite a surprise to me. I had never seen them detailed to that extent, and it made me wonder if our charge of aggression on the part of the North Vietnamese might not be a case of the pot calling the kettle black.

REP. ECKHARDT: I have a question about the Papers themselves. First, I understand that the little volume that has been published is a publication of those portions of the Papers that were published. That is correct, isn't it?

REP. DOW: That is correct.

REP. ECKHARDT: In the trials both in New York and here, there was reference, as I recall, to eleven so-called sensitive documents. At any rate, we were not permitted to see those, even though we sought to intervene in the lawsuit, because these were considered *in camera*, and the list of them was even submitted as a sealed document.

I am not clear whether these items are items covered in the published papers or whether they are wholly in the unpublished portion or whether they lap over into both groups. I wondered if anyone here might have any information on that matter to clear up that point.

I don't know what was classified as sensitive. The case of Near *versus* Minnesota states that the only thing that may possibly be subject to a prior restraint is that which is of the nature of giving information regarding troop ship movements in

[3 2]

time of war, the location of massing of troops and things of that description.

So it is very difficult for anyone to use the published documents to determine whether they fall within the definition of sensitive material as set forth in Near *versus* Minnesota. And it is very difficult even for Congressmen who have access to the complete set of documents to know precisely what is referred to.

Perhaps Mr. Ellsberg could comment on whether or not any of these Papers do appear to be within the Near *versus* Minnesota exception. The court says they are not, but we have no way presently of obtaining any guidance, even if we have access to the full Papers, as to what these various items, named by the Solicitor General as sensitive matters actually are.

I would like to know what they are, at least as a guideline. I do have access to the Papers as a Member of Congress, but it is pretty difficult to search through vast numbers of pages without any indication of what the government is pointing out as such sensitive material.

DR. ELLSBERG: I sympathize with your problem because, to my knowledge, no page of the material meets those criteria. I am not privy to what the government claimed these items were.

It is a question of what the Defense Department and the Justice Department claim is sensitive material, since, I believe, this claim was limited to two district-court judges who ruled against it in their opinion.

But it would seem to me that Congress will have to make some decision on how to deal with these documents and when and how to make them available to the public. It will surely be interesting to learn, when such information is revealed, what, in the opinion of the government and the Executive sensitive material is.

[33]

I read in the paper that Secretary Rogers had offered to give his opinion on this matter to the press. I don't know whether the media availed themselves of this statement, but I should think Congress would want to see that list.

REP. ECKHARDT: I would like to know what was on those lists which were delivered *in camera*. I would be willing to accept them under any limitations or conditions, because it seems to me that unless one knows the nature of the material, to merely riffle through thousands of pages of paper is a rather fruitless and difficult means of determining what our policy was with respect to classification.

DR. ELLSBERG: Has Congress not asked the Executive for that information?

REP. EDWARDS: We took a vote on the floor of the House and were defeated. The vote was on whether or not all of the volumes would be made available to all of us and we were voted down in the House of Representatives.

REP. CONYERS: It is difficult for us to keep looking at the Pentagon Papers as if they contained secret messages.

The Pentagon Papers confirm what many of us suspected even before their revelation. After listening to all of the speakers here, I am moved deeply by a single theme.

We must somehow politicize those persons who have joined us today here in the audience and who are representative of, I hope, millions of other Americans.

We must become more than the best-informed people on the horrors of war, on the failure of the Pentagon and this government. The question is ultimately, "What are we going to do about it?"

If we look at the two-party system, then this faceless Con-

[34]

gress divides into Democrats and Republicans: in the House, 255 Democrats and 179 Republicans; in the Senate, fifty-five Democrats and forty-five Republicans.

The question then becomes: "What are we going to do about those among us who may be supporting those programs and policies we find so abhorrent?" What I am suggesting is that we begin to recognize the realities of our two-party system: that the leaders of both parties have supported continuing the war. They have destroyed the chance of making the United States a viable community, of ending racism and of creating full employment. We must seriously re-evaluate the two-party, no-choice system.

Yes, we are here to discuss the Pentagon Papers, but more than that, we are here to highlight the need for the massive reforms that are due the American people and have been due them since the beginning of the twentieth century.

REP. DOW: I think that we might merge the question that Congressman Eckhardt has raised with the general question raised by Congressman Conyers by asking the question, "How can we increase the oversight of Congress on the Executive?"

What can we do to reassert Congressional control and how should it be done? Should we have a much stronger audit function which would ultimately result in our constant surveillance of Executive performance?

How can Congress and the Executive relate to each other in situations like Vietnam and the Pentagon Papers so that the ghastly mistakes borne of that relationship in the past are not perpetuated in the future? Would any of the conference participants care to comment on that question?

REP. CONYERS: One way is to seek a Congressional leadership that really wants to reassert Congressional control—if

[35]

indeed it ever existed. It is very clear to me that we do not have that kind of leadership presently in the House.

For us to come here and sit and worry about this as if it were some abstract question is a little disturbing to me because it is very clear that, outside of the few Members gathered here and a few others not present there is no distinct desire on the part of our leadership to further that end.

How did the leadership evolve? Most of us (and many liberals joined with conservatives) helped to put them in the offices that they now use to frustrate us. Hence, it seems to me, we come inescapably back to the need for politicizing those liberals in the Congress and those citizens concerned with this question so that we can begin to create an atmosphere in which we can honestly examine the question that you raised.

I don't think we can do that at this point.

REP. RYAN: I should like to say to Mr. Ellsberg that he has brought to public awareness the manipulations, secrecy and deceptions which were practiced all during the Vietnam period, all the way back to 1950. The revelations of the Pentagon Papers are important to furthering an understanding of the role of the United States in Southeast Asia.

There must be a re-examination of our entire foreign policy. We were united in World War II as a country behind the President to win a world war. Politics stopped at the water's edge. It was a bipartisan effort.

What happened after World War II was a continuation of the concept of bipartisanship in foreign policy without any seriously critical opposition. Whether it was President Truman with Dean Acheson, President Eisenhower with John Foster Dulles or President Kennedy or Johnson with Dean Rusk, the assumptions underlying our foreign policy from the end of World War II were basically the same.

The Congress did not challenge, but rather reinforced those assumptions, of which the Vietnam war was a logical extension. It was believed to be essential to draw a line in Asia against expanding monolithic Communism. Therefore, a containment policy to prevent the so-called dominoes from falling was pursued.

During the period of the Vietnam war the Congress abdicated to the Executive branch, although there were some of us at this table who raised our voices in opposition to the war and fought against Vietnam war appropriations. In view of the failure of the Congress to exercise restraint on the Executive, is there any hope that we can examine the structure of the Executive branch and build in any checks and balances? That's one question.

Then there is the question of the extent to which the military, during this period, came to dominate the diplomats. What do the Pentagon Papers show in that respect? It appears that the military had indeed been dominating the diplomats during this period.

I think we really ought to explore all these questions. Perhaps, Dr. Ellsberg, you might address yourself to the question of whether or not there is any hope of building checks into the system?

DR. ELLSBERG: I wouldn't put my trust in a lot of checks within the Executive branch in hopes that the Executive will always remain responsive to the President's desires and the desires of Congress. Congress has to use its power to assert its own role. I have come to appreciate, in the last several months more than ever before, the wisdom of the signers of the Constitution in providing for parallel responsibilities and for some independence in various branches of government.

People ask whether, after all, those in the Executive branch

[37]

are the only ones who can be corrupted by power and who shirk responsibility. Obviously not. We are talking about a generation of behavior, very similar behavior demonstrated by a large number of people, and that in itself almost proves that it is not the character of any one person that is to be judged by the performance of a system, nor is it the kind of people that go into the Executive branch.

Such people as Nixon, Laird, Johnson, Truman and Kennedy all came from Congress. In fact, I saw in the papers that Richard Nixon protested strongly the holding by Truman of certain documents during that period.

These same people could have been relied on twenty years ago, a little earlier in the cold war at least, to oppose the kind of behavior that the Executive is foreseeably showing right now.

In other words, I think one has to address Congress's will to provide a check on the Executive; the same applies to the courts. But we are in the halls of Congress now, and let's take it from there. Congress has, in effect, signed over its responsibilities under the Constitution in the field of war and foreign policy, for over twenty-five years, and I think you are exactly right in attributing this to the legacy of World War II.

The definition of the situation we are in as a cold war has had fateful consequences on the functioning of our constitutional system and our democracy. This is a perception that all of us share.

A vivid lesson was provided by the four years of our participation in World War II. It became apparent that our affairs in the world were to be conducted by the President. Congress virtually went to sleep. The courts abjured responsibility.

Citizens and Congress together were to accept measures of censorship, in effect, the concealing of information. To define the situation and encourage the analogy of the World War II

struggle for survival against the powerful opponent, would seem to answer all these questions of whether the Executive had the right to assume such vast responsibility.

In a way, I think Congress has to make the mental and emotional effort to escape from the power of these metaphors and analogies with World War II, from the experiences that shaped people like Richard Nixon—who was a junior officer in that war—like so many others who see the world in those terms. Congress must help us return to peace and tell the people of this country it is within our power to bring about peace in our relationship to the rest of the world.

It is not within our power to end all violence in the world, but it is within our power to abandon the wartime distribution of power which places all responsibility and all power in the hands of the Executive.

REP. ECKHARDT: I have a question I would like to ask Dr. Ellsberg. We have been discussing this question of information available to the people and to Congress. It is my assumption that once information is available to the press there should be almost no restraint.

Nevertheless, there is the other question of to what extent the Executive should retain material privately and for what period of time. In other words, I think there is a difference between the cat in the bag and the cat out of the bag.

I don't think many of us would say that we must know currently and absolutely and immediately details of the conduct of foreign relations. Yet I think we would also agree that the retention of materials, particularly those having more to do with policy making than defense, should never have been held as long as the Pentagon Papers were.

Is there some guideline as to where we should draw those lines? I don't assume that you would say, for instance, we

should necessarily have known step by step what Mr. Kissinger was doing in preparation for the China trip. Yet I would think the retention of information concerning important matters of policy for a period of twenty years, or even for a period of three or four years, is a deviation from a sound practice.

Now where do we draw that line?

MR. RASKIN: I think Senator Fulbright put his finger on the problem when he said that Congress should have been informed of such a major change in policy, and indeed, should have been involved at least to the extent of its constitutional capacity. When states conduct their business in secret, surprising their "audience" may be amusing to leaders, but the people are still the ones who must carry the rifles and suffer the consequences of their leaders' decisions.

So, in that sense, it would seem to me perfectly sensible that congressional involvement in decision making is crucial. Constitutionally this power cannot be relinquished.

Dr. Kissinger's going to China may be good or may be bad ideologically, depending on one's point of view, but it doesn't deal with the structural question.

I would argue that congressional responsibility would virtually demand that Congress be involved in one form or another.

REP. ECKHARDT: Yes, but I think, at least generally, the constitutional concepts do envisage the Executive branch conducting foreign relations. It would seem to me that an absolute, immediate and current involvement with Congress would bog down international relations interminably.

MR. RASKIN: I think that in terms of the Papers and in terms of the question of whether vested interests can be built

[40]

into the government, we have some interesting examples of where such attempts were made.

The Arms Control and Disarmament Agency is a case in point. It was designed as a vested interest for disarmament and has been in existence now for some ten years. I don't think its results are very promising insofar as it relates to the power of the Department of Defense.

The idea that you are able to have a friend in court, so to speak, has, at best, a marginal utility and won't do very much good. On the other hand, it would seem to me that what we are really talking about is not so much the question of defeat or foreign policy conducted in private, but rather behavior and the limits of behavior—that is to say, what it is that people who are in positions of power can or can not do. Now it seems to me the task of the legislature is to legislate on the conduct and behavior of bureaucrats, such as was done in the case of the Hatch Act.

Looked at another way, if it is true that there is a stricture against taking bribes, it may very well be that there ought to be a stricture against bureaucrats or policy makers undertaking aggressive wars on their own, or planning for them, or dropping nuclear weapons, or undertaking covert activities against other nations.

Indeed, we must not only be concerned about bribe-taking in the federal government or wherever it may take place, but we must consider the consequences of Congressional setting of rules within constitutional parameters which prohibit any action outside those rules and setting penalties for such breaches.

In this sense, there would be some clarification as to what we expect of major government officials and what we view as their responsibility. This is what has been attempted under the Uniform Code of Military Justice for the military, which, although imperfect, is nonetheless an important document.

[41]

There is no reason why a civilian code should not apply to civilians in the government, to civilian bureaucrats who undertake to make decisions affecting national security and foreign policy matters. Otherwise, there is no way indeed that Congress will ever be able to establish limits on Executive frolics or even be consulted about them.

The history of the twentieth century shows that the larger a central government becomes, the greater its administrative power and, conversely, the less powerful its legislature.

Therefore, the only way we can redress that balance, especially in the context of national security and foreign policy, is by laying out a list of proscribed activities for government officials.

REP. CONYERS: The majority of the American people don't want war. The Gallup poll clearly shows this. Hence the question is: "How do we get the elected government to stop committing the American people to war?"

How do we begin to recognize that these criticisms, dating back over thirty years, address themselves to a failure of liberal politics in the United States? We are not talking about the reactionaries. We are not talking about the racists. We are not isolating the southern members of the Congress.

We are talking about facing up now to the problems that were created by "liberal, idealistic, well-intentioned" members of a government. This is the more difficult problem that we have to face. We must ask ourselves how we can move an intransigent Congress.

What do we say to a President who doesn't speak clearly to the seven-point peace proposal? It is not a matter of harnessing the Executive, but rather a question of addressing ourselves to an administration and a Congress that are equally unresponsive.

So, I want to ask us to begin to think about how we politicize those of us in government. How do we motivate our citizenry to man the political barricades, as it were, to bring about the atmosphere where questions such as these can be honestly entertained?

MR. BRANFMAN: I would like to speak directly to that point because I think Representative Conyers has touched on what is really the key question facing us right now. I think that we have got to face the basic reality. This is that as a consequence of proliferation of technology which has taken place since World War II, the centralization of economic power and numerous psychological factors, the Executive branch in this country today controls the power, the technology and the funds for our foreign ventures and, of course, for many of our domestic policies in a way that makes it impossible for Congress to act.

It is easy, I think, to talk in theory about what Congress as a body can do. There are a hundred things, starting with cutting off funds tomorrow for the war in Indochina, refusing to fund any foreign ventures that Congress hasn't been consulted about or placing members of Congress in embassies all over the world on a full-time basis to monitor activities of the Executive branch.

Thus to talk about what Congress can do in theory does not present a problem. The problem is to talk about what can be done practically, in the present context.

We must face the facts. These are more war casualties now than before. It is true that we have drawn out several thousand troops and will be drawing out more. Our troops are being taken out of active combat roles. Nonetheless, in that the bombing is being escalated, more and more civilians are dying. I have interviewed several thousand refugees in the last

two years. I have talked to countless others who have had their children burned to death, put to death before their eyes, countless wives who have lost their husbands in the same fashion.

This kind of thing is documented in the Senate subcommittee report. We have dropped 2,200,000 tons of bombs since Nixon came into office. That is more than was dropped on all of Europe in World War II.

The Pentagon Papers have created a very special situation in this country. There is probably no one in this room who failed to criticize the Germans in World War II during the 1930's. I think what the Pentagon Papers have done is to place all of us in precisely that situation. Now there are many things that can be done by individual Congressmen which will ameliorate the situation somewhat, such as asking for the release of more of the Pentagon Papers. But it seems to me that given the present situation what is necessary is for individual Congressmen to begin to take action which goes beyond the forms that have taken place in the past.

I propose that individual Congressmen go to Southeast Asia and demand that they be allowed on forward air control flights, not for a day, not for a special flight which can be staged, but for a few weeks. Perhaps the Senate Foreign Relations Committee could station people in Southeast Asia with access to reports. I see Congressmen going to Saigon and standing next to Huynh Tan Mam during his trial and making sure that whatever happens during it will be known by the whole world. I see Congressmen going to Laos and demanding to be taken to the heroin factories which are sending heroin to our boys in Vietnam. (There was an article by Flora Lewis[4] last week on an interview with the head of a Pentagon task

---

[4] *Washington Post*, July 23, 1971.

force on heroin intake by United States troops. Quite frankly, the gist of the interview was that we know where the heroin factories are. We know they are in Laos, but we won't take action because the generals we are supporting there won't let us fight our war if we do.) There are a hundred things that individual Congressmen can do to raise the level of consciousness in this country.

Second, of course, when Congressmen do take such action it is necessary for all of us to support them and to do everything we can to raise the consciousness of our own communities.

I think that all of us must measure up to the standard set by Daniel Ellsberg. We should remember every moment that at the rate the bombs have been falling since the first of this year, 350 million more tons will fall before the end of the year—that is two thousand tons every hour.

This means that in the two hours we have been here, four thousand tons of bombs have fallen on Indochina, have killed people, burned them with napalm, cut them to pieces and buried them alive. We must bear this in mind and act accordingly.

PROF. MARR: I would like to follow up on Fred Branfman's remarks. I think, if the Congressmen are going to take such action, they not only have to make the moral commitment to go out in the field and accomplish what he has indicated, but they have to be given sufficient informational input to know where to go, when to go, how to go and who and what to see.

A perfect example of this is Don Luce's visit to the Tiger Cages in Con Son. He was accompanied by two Congressmen and had a map which was provided by students. This is the only reason they could see what they saw.

[45]

Such experiences indicate that Congress must have much greater access to information than it currently has. I am frankly amazed that Congress has been so meek in depending upon the State Department, the Pentagon and other official agencies for their sources of information.

Why don't you finance yourself and provide independent sources of information?

MR. RASKIN: I wonder, though, at this stage, what new information is needed to make either a political, moral or legal judgment about the Indochina war?

PROF. MARR: It is not the judgment that is necessary but the ammunition. I gave the example of the Tiger Cages. This is a way of counterpunching the administration with factual evidence.

We made the judgment. We have taken our position. We have to have the ammunition in order to fight with it.

MR. RASKIN: But that, again, assumes that factual evidence really makes a difference.

MR. HOSTETTER: I think the exposure of the Pentagon Papers has been an excellent example of the fact that it *does not* make a difference. Now, although every American in the United States either knows or has access to those facts indicating that we are fighting an illegal, unjust, immoral and unlawful war, yet the war continues.

I think we have to stop talking about information and declassifying more information. I think we have enough information right now to act. I think Mr. Branfman has come to the crux of the problem. We are now in the same situation that the Germans were in, and unless we take a stronger course of

[46]

action than the Germans did at that time, we will be under the same moral condemnation that they were under.

Perhaps Dr. Ellsberg could speak to this point. Perhaps the time has come when working strictly within the system and following the rules that have been set up by that system are not enough.

REP. ECKHARDT: Isn't that really irrelevant to how one acts as a Congressman? You have almost got to assume that there is some effective role for a Congressman within the system.

It seems to me, the place for a Congressman is not in Saigon, but say, in Houston, Texas. It seems to me that there is a considerable lag between available information and knowledge in a group like this, for instance, and that available to the people at large in any area where the sources of information are not so accessible.

The publication of the Pentagon Papers brought information to people through a responsible and, in the eyes of the people, reputable source. But I don't see that we do much good as individual Congressmen, who are already convinced, by making spectacular gestures like going off somewhere in pursuit of knowledge which we already have.

MR. RASKIN: Congressman, I don't want to be understood as suggesting that this is what you should do. I think you should act in your role of Congressman. I would think, from a citizen's point of view, that the Congress must set down a code of criminal and noncriminal behavior for government officials, which in effect says there are certain things officials cannot do in their governmental capacity. As you know, my conclusion is that much of the war is criminal and the Pentagon Papers make out a *prima facie* case that the war is an aggressive one.

[47]

On that basis, you must start from those international laws that define criminal behavior. If, on the other hand, you don't think that covert operations are criminal, if it is the case that the bombings and the population removal programs are acceptable—that, in fact, they do reflect the point of view of the Congress of the United States because the majority of that Congress vote funds for these programs—then Congress is complicitous. If so, then Congress has been collaborating with a system which, in fact, is a system of crimes that were laid down as such in the period of 1945 to 1947 by the United States government.

Congressman Kowalski is here. My recollection is that during the period 1945–1946, he was a member of the United States military government in Japan, and I think it would be very useful to hear from him about what the standards were then, what the United States government demanded of the Japanese and the Japanese government in terms of the prevailing militarism and ultranationalism.

COL. KOWALSKI: Japan, as all of you know, was the extreme, ugly pit of militarism and ultranationalism. After the war, when we occupied the country, the United States forced upon the Japanese the greatest peacetime revolution the world has seen. In a devastating blow we knocked out—purged—the militarists and their allies in industry and politics. Anyone remotely connected with the conduct of the war was eliminated from positions of influence in the nation.

And so, as I look at our current operations in Vietnam and Southeast Asia, I can hardly believe that twenty-five years ago, it was the United States army that brought democracy to Japan. Under the Supreme Commander, General Douglas MacArthur, our military forced upon the Japanese nation a great humanitarian land reform, gave women the right to vote and

initiated reforms in the judiciary, public welfare and education. Moreover, United States army officers actually helped Japanese workers to organize labor unions. Most significantly, we should never forget that a general of the United States gave Japan a constitution (the only one in the world) that bans all military forces in the nation and forsakes war forever. (Albeit, to save our necks in the Korean war, we trampled upon that constitution.) In Japan, our contributions to humanity were tremendous. We can be proud of what our army accomplished there. Most of all we can be proud of the progressive national policies that initiated those programs. The United States can do great things—if she wants to.

Having said these kind words about the military and our past national policies, I would like to address myself to Congressman Conyer's basic question: "What can Congress do about the problems under discussion?" More specifically, I should like to limit myself to an inherent aspect of that question: "What can Congress do about our growing militarism?" "What can we do about controlling the military?"

The military establishment of the United States has grown into a Frankenstein. Its power pervades the globe. With our forces stationed all over the world, our foreign policy is totally dependent upon the will of the men who command and manage this huge machine. Foreign governments are subverted, military dictatorships supported, while billions of dollars worth of Pentagon munitions are being peddled to friends throughout the world who were trained in our military schools. On the domestic side, our military requirements and budgets dominate our economy. Whole industries exist to feed the monster. The insatiable need for military hardware provides jobs for our workers, while the hungry demands for increasing numbers of young men invade the lives of millions of our families.

[49]

This power rests upon the ability of the military to extract an ever larger chunk of the tax dollar from Congress. They have been able to exact this immense tribute because they have penetrated and subverted the civilian power structure of the nation.

In some measure the military establishment enjoys this power because Congress and the political leaders of our country are awed by the Pentagon. I am sorry to say that many of the problems experienced by President Kennedy in Cuba, in Vietnam, in control of nuclear armaments stemmed from his great awe of the men in uniform. A national chairman of the Democratic party once told me in discussing our disaster in Vietnam: "We thought, Frank, your buddies in the Pentagon knew what they were doing." Well, I have news for him—they don't know what they're doing!

Congress can curb the military in many ways without creating difficulties or operational problems for the sincere conscientious officers in our services. Fundamental control of the military rests in the administration, but under the Constitution of the United States, Congress is the board of directors of our military establishment. The Constitution specifically assigns to Congress the power "to make rules for the government and regulation of the land and naval forces."

Hence, the first item on the agenda for Congress, and specifically for our own distinguished group of Congressmen, should be to get the military out of politics. Essentially this is the responsibility of our military committees in Congress. In view of the leadership of those committees, it is doubtful that any curbs will be initiated there. Accordingly, it may be necessary for a group of Congressmen, again perhaps our own group, to form a committee for the purpose of investigating the military in politics and to explore action necessary to curb the political power of our military. In the meantime it would

seem to me that each Congressman should make it his personal responsibility to stop any man in uniform who speaks out publicly on a political issue whether it relates to international or domestic matters.

Another important area where Congress can exercise more effective control over the military is through the operation of the Code of Military Justice. Without elaborating, I would urge this group of Congressmen to join in the efforts now developing to review and revise the present Code. They should especially direct their attention to the responsibilities and accountability of military commanders for conduct of operations against civilian populations, hopefully placing limits on bombing authority vested in the military, defining limits to planning for war and exploiting the emotions of our own citizenry in the service of war.

An especially critical area where our military must be curbed is that of strategic military planning. The Pentagon Papers are truly frightening in terms of their implications about the plans and planning of the military for war, contingencies and annihilation. Under the assumption that the military is best qualified to plan for war, and given the view of the military that it knows what's best for the country, we have developed horrendous national suicidal programs. It is precisely in strategic military planning—in every element of it—that civilians should assume direct control of our national plans—not just oversight but day-to-day participation in the planning. Specifically, there should be no strategic military planning carried on solely by military men.

Finally, because time is limited, as an immediate small step in the direction of demilitarizing the Pentagon, I recommend that our distinguished group of Congressmen urge the President to make a provision whereby all servicemen and women on duty in the Pentagon are taken out of uniform. You'd be

[51]

pleasantly surprised to see how ordinary a four-star general or admiral looks in civilian dress.

DR. ELLSBERG: I have two thoughts. One, I am struck listening to you, Congressman Kowalski, because of your special background. I was thinking over the various presidents you were talking about earlier, the ones who ignored, bypassed, lied to, and, in general, treated the Congress almost contemptuously.

These were the presidents in wartime affairs, namely, Truman, Johnson, Kennedy and Nixon, who came from Congress. Interestingly, the one president who took Congress's role in these matters quite seriously, and in fact, let Congress impose what amounted to a veto—an effective veto—and kept us away from the disastrous possibility of going into North Vietnam, was Eisenhower—listening, in part, to such people as Lyndon Johnson in the Congress.

The irony continues when one considers that Eisenhower had a military background, and that his skepticism was reserved for the Joint Chiefs of Staff, which he repeatedly tried to abolish while Congress repeatedly came to their aid. He was distrustful of the Joint Chiefs as an institution in the command process.

The question for Congressmen, it occurs to me, is what do you regard as the right of the Executive to lie directly to you?

Putting it the other way, what do you regard as your responsibilities to your constituents under the Constitution when an Executive official—and we are not talking only of the President but also of the appointed officials under him—comes before a Congressional committee and not only, on the one hand, conceals information—as clearly happened before the Cambodian invasion—but also lies about what happened, as in

connection with the Cambodian invasion, the Laotian invasion and the Son Tay raid?

I happened to be in Washington when Secretary Laird appeared before the Fulbright Committee for, I think, the second time, partly in connection with the Son Tay raid. It is perfectly evident from the information that came out in the newspapers that Secretary Laird made untrue statements about what we had done on the outskirts of Hanoi in connection with that raid in the firing of rockets—a war time act against another country. The American people had to learn directly about that from Hanoi Radio, which naturally at first didn't have a great deal of plausibility.

I fully expected to witness the panel of Senators confronting Secretary Laird jump down his throat. Presumably he hadn't carried out this mission on his own initiative, but still he had carried it out.

On the contrary, I think, if anything, the Senators were on the defensive in this exchange. This kind of thing happens again and again, and I wonder why it is regarded as almost heresy to talk about impeachment as Representative McCloskey has.

One needn't start with the President. There are Secretaries of Defense, the Air Force and the Army, who from time to time are in a position of deliberately misleading Congress.

We do have the case of Cambodia in which the President informed the people in a public speech that the intelligence estimates indicated that North Vietnamese troops were massing for the purpose of going west into South Vietnam, thereby endangering our troops.

That was an untrue statement later abandoned by the administration. Again, I heard almost no criticism from Congress. In short, Congress seems always to be acting out this role of helplessness and lack of legitimate right and need to

know, which I can not believe is in the service of its constituents.

REP. ECKHARDT: Frequently we don't know whether it is a lie or not because we don't know if it has been misrepresented until much later. As I mentioned earlier, there is a current situation regarding the atomic experiment in the Aleutians that is scheduled to come off in October of this year and this is related to the question posed by Dr. Ellsberg.

We shall vote on appropriations for this experiment on July 29. If at the time of the vote, Congresswoman Mink is still denied access to the reports she has been requesting of the Executive branch, there is one thing we as Members of Congress can do. We can simply refuse to vote on the appropriations until we have reasonable candor from the President. I think that is the most effective thing we can do.

REP. ROSENTHAL: I think Dr. Ellsberg knew the answers to the questions he raised. He really raised them to gain a dialogue. I probably am the most senior conference person around here, having participated in these conferences with Brothers Raskin, Ryan, Dow and others since 1965.

We began these meetings in 1965, with Bernie Fall, Marc Raskin and many others who told us about the savagery of the war, our inability to win it, and its basic immorality.

No one here has really addressed himself to the major question. You keep asking why we don't do this and why we don't do that. Until you address yourself to the question of institutional change in Congress, nothing can be done.

If the Pentagon Papers, as Marc has just suggested to me, had been on the front page of *The New York Times* for the past ten years, honestly, it would have made no difference because Congress has become a feeble second-class citizen vis-a-vis the Executive for all the reasons that someone sug-

gested here—including the advancement of technology and the reverence for the presidency.

We may not, as individuals, have a relationship with the President, but there is a kind of awe for the "royalty" of the presidency. The President also has an incredible ability to fly the flag when the situation gets difficult.

As one who voted for the Gulf of Tonkin Resolution, President Johnson flew the flag and caused the bands to play their martial music. My committee, the Foreign Affairs Committee, spent exactly sixty minutes discussing the Gulf of Tonkin.

Somewhat later, we learned that we had been lied to left, right and sidewise about it, but what were we to do? The answer is, nothing, until we remove the moat that surrounds this building.

This is the only place in the United States where someone like myself—now forty-eight years old—is described as a young, dynamic Congressman. This place is not geared to accommodate itself to the changes and needs of society and the United States. This place is not built to challenge anybody. Our institutions and our committee structures all operate with inadequate staff. On the other hand, we are kept quite comfortable in this building, with its really splendid isolation. So the major question is not what we would do if the Secretary lied and we found out about it although this is a matter we have to address ourselves to. But, rather the major question should be, if we are going to make this nation responsive to its needs and its role in society, how can we build a viable and co-equal legislative branch, as the framers of the Constitution originally intended?

Most members of Congress do accept their constitutional role of casually inquiring about foreign policy, but they don't feel themselves adequate to challenge the authoritarian decisions that the Executive makes.

So, while we are all raising such questions as: do you respond to a Secretary if he lies, or should Congressmen see that he is punished, the answers to those questions are obviously yes. Should we preserve a constitutionally mandated law? The answer to that question is obviously yes. Should we have a conference like this again next year? Again, the answer is obviously yes. That would be my fifth conference and we are still dropping more bombs per square inch in Vietnam than ever before.

What ought to come out of this conference is a clear plea—not a mandate—but a plea to the American people to rise up and say, if the Congress can't be a meaningful institution—I hesitate to say this—we should go home and let it be abolished.

Many, if not a majority of the members of this House, are very competent people whether this is understood or not. But the institutional structure with the seniority system imposed from the top inhibits a representative from doing the job his people expect him to do.

There again, I would suggest that what must come out of this conference is a clear understanding of where we are with regard to the war in Indochina, the necessity for immediate termination and the consideration of some kind of censure action against the President if he continues these policies.

We cannot go into the 1970's, 1980's, and 1990's and face the 200th anniversary of this republic unless we are willing to make major, drastic alterations in the system we now know as the Congress of the United States.

REP. SEIBERLING: I simply want to add a few words to the very effective and eloquent statement Mr. Rosenthal has made. I am a freshman and I am fifty-two years old, and I am

suffering from the cultural shock of coming to this institution from no previous political office.

One of the first things I discovered—I knew it intellectually but I discovered it in my own experience—was the fact that Congress is representative in form, but it is not a representative body in fact because of the very reasons Mr. Rosenthal has mentioned.

All Congressmen are not created equal. The Congress is ruled by a very small minority and that's it. Unfortunately, that very minority, in the pursuit of its own personal power, has abdicated the power of Congress as a whole.

What we are faced with is basically a grave constitutional crisis in this country, and I think that the Pentagon Papers have brought out, in the most dramatic way, the extent to which the Executive branch is running the whole show in substance, not only in disregard of the Congress but in disregard of the public.

I feel that we must do more than dramatize the extent to which we need reform in Congress. We must see to it that the American public arrives at a basic understanding that we do have a crisis because the Congress of the United States, which was created for their protection, is not performing its full function.

Rather than a drastic revolution in Congress, in the sense of a constitutional change in structure, what we really need to do is get back to the original concept of what this body was supposed to do.

The means for doing this has been debated at great length in Congress and to some extent in the country. I simply hope that we can get across to the rest of the people in this country that this is a crisis which affects them to the very core and they are in a position to demand that the Congress go back to its original concepts.

[57]

If we can do that we will have achieved far more than pin-pointing blame on individuals for some of the events in the past, because we are all involved and implicated in this to some extent or another.

REP. ECKHARDT: I don't think things are quite as bad as has been indicated. The very fact that people are now beginning to look at the misrepresentations and the false bases for some of our actions in the past; the fact that the Supreme Court supported free speech prohibiting prior restraint; the fact that today there is a platform for the kind of expression that is occurring here; the fact that in Congress there is, for the first time in several sessions, the revitalization of the Democratic caucus, which is the only machinery I know of that establishes a base of responsibility in general for the position of the party which is a majority party and the more liberal party in Congress; all of these factors suggest that the current picture is not so terribly discouraging as it might appear. I think we are perfectly right to probe deeply into what is wrong with Congress, into what is wrong with the falsifications that Congress has received and to try to devise means by which Congress can be apprised of the facts in sufficient time to make effective decisions.

But I certainly don't look at the situation that exists now as wholly discouraging and I do think we are moving in a proper direction.

REP. ROSENTHAL: Let me have a moment to respond just to that. Those are very sincere and eloquent remarks from my friend from Texas. But honestly, Bob, I don't take much comfort in the fact that we are having another conference now or that we currently have 152 or 167 votes, because the situation has become a hundred times worse.

[58]

We have continued the war all these years. I can't take much comfort in these things which I say are valid, useful and important because we are nonetheless, with all these improvements, perpetuating the kind of war we have been involved in for essentially twenty years.

We have gone five yards and there are ninety-five yards more to go.

REP. KOCH: Everything that Ben Rosenthal and Bob Eckhardt and the others have said is obviously factual and should be supported, but I want to say I don't think that the blame can be shifted exactly that way.

Congress reflects the fact that less than fifty per cent of the people in this country go to the polls. Now, whose fault is that? This is not the fault of the Congress. It is the fault of the electorate.

There are areas in this country where members of Congress have no opposition at all. There is not even a member of the other party running against them, so in point of fact there is no contest.

Then there are larger areas of the country where members of Congress are elected by an electorate which is composed of less than fifty per cent of those eligible to vote. Do you know that New York City comes under the Voting Rights law because less than fifty per cent of the voting-age public went to the polls in the appropriate year? New Yorkers are thus under the same blanket, as it were, that the Southern states are.

This is rightfully so, but it isn't because there is an imposition of obstacles on the part of the city or state government which prevents people from voting. It just happens that people aren't voting.

MR. RASKIN: Why do you think they are not?

REP. KOCH: Some might say that the percentage of non-voters is so high because people are fed up, but I don't think that is true at all because they weren't voting when there was nothing to be fed up about. They haven't been voting for years and years. Why it is, I don't know, but it seems to me that if people are really going to become more involved in government something must be done about getting them to register and vote.

Registration is taking place in New York City today, yet there are very few who are taking advantage of the fact that if you are eighteen you can register to vote. Something has got to be changed, and it is the people who will have to change it.

REP. RYAN: In commenting upon what has been said by my colleagues, let me say that I agree with Bob Eckhardt. I am very concerned. However, there are changes in the wind. It is apparent, judging by the response to the House equivalent of the Hatfield-McGovern amendment—176 votes in this session of the Congress[5]—that our strength has increased since 1965 when only a handful of us opposed the war. Yet, the fact remains that the war continues. The death and destruction continue. The Constitution is still being violated. The war is conducted through presidential exercise of the war-making power, a function which supposedly has been reserved for Congress.

It is essential that there be a change in the institutional structure of the Congress itself. There is no question about it. At the same time, it seems to me that we have to develop some means whereby internal checks and balances within the Executive branch can be provided.

[5] The vote referred to took place in the House June 28, 1971. The 176 votes were against tabling a motion made by Rep. Whalen (R-Ohio) to instruct the House conferees on the draft extension bill to accept the wording of the Mansfield amendment. The motion was tabled.

Mr. Raskin talks about the Arms Control and Disarmament Agency. At first, when we introduced the legislation, we called it a peace agency. However, the name "peace agency" had to be changed to gain support in Congress. Mr. Kowalski was one of the original sponsors of that bill back in 1961 and 1962.

Let us see what the Pentagon Papers show regarding the need for internal checks and balances. I think it is an important question.

DR. ELLSBERG: I can't entirely agree with the present preoccupation with the question of institutional change and of changing the relations between Congress and the Executive.

I think structural change is needed, obviously, and I think the Pentagon Papers are relevant to the kinds of changes that are necessary. I certainly hope that the Pentagon Papers will contribute, over a matter of years, to constructive changes by showing how urgently and in what areas they are needed.

But that won't end the war as quickly as it must be ended. Institutional change, which will take years, I think, cannot be relied upon. Nor, in fact, can presidential electoral politics be relied upon to end this war or our involvement in the war before we have carried out certain recent policies, as in Cambodia and Laos, to their implied conclusion, and destroyed North Vietnam.

I have thought for some time that it is essential to adddress ourselves to the shorter-run question. How do we bring the war to an end before the United States adopts the policy of destroying North Vietnam?

As I look around at the elements of our society that might end it and could end it, I have to focus on Congress. Moreover, I have to focus on individual Congressmen doing "unconventional" things.

THE PRESS: Dr. Ellsberg, while you were at it with the various interesting Pentagon Papers, if you had the Gulf of Tonkin incident study, why didn't you release it? Did you have access to it?

DR. ELLSBERG: I did have access to it at one time. In fact, in 1964, during a study under Walter Rostow, an interagency study of crisis decision-making, I was the only civilian outside of the Weapons System Evaluation Group of IDA, which had done these crisis studies, to be given official access. I spent part of that year reading all of the crisis studies that were done, including their command and control study.

That was a period when the Secretary of Defense did not have access to the study, nor did he have access to that study until Senator Fulbright asked him for it in 1968. The testimony of the Secretary of Defense in 1968 shows he commented quite correctly that he had never heard of this study until a few days before Senator Fulbright had asked him for it. I am well aware of the fact that he was telling the truth when he said that.

THE PRESS: Having read the study, Dr. Ellsberg, what do you feel it tells us about the origin of the American escalation of the war?

DR. ELLSBERG: The command and control study? It doesn't add much now. Of course, when it was written, it was in direct contradiction to many of the statements made by Secretary McNamara before the Fulbright Committee and before Congress voted on the Tonkin Gulf Resolution.

This is one of the things I thought Congressman Eckhardt might be interested in. He raised the question about where one draws the line on what is released and what isn't released, the assumption being that the line could not possibly or re-

sponsibly be drawn more liberally than the released Pentagon Papers indicate.

Of course nothing in those documents is more recent than three years ago. I would question whether that is the standard one must go by. I think most Congressmen have indicated that they feel it would be impossible, under any circumstances, to demand or receive material, for instance, on covert operations occurring at the time, or shortly afterwards, or on current operations.

Now I would certainly dispute that. President Kennedy's comments to *The New York Times* in 1962, the year after the Bay of Pigs, were that he wished they had revealed, at the time, the covert operation of the Bay of Pigs.

This was a presidential judgment, a very reasonable one: that the public would have been better served if Congress had had that information. About the command and control study you mentioned, the information contained in that would have dealt with the so-called 34A operations against North Vietnam being conducted in the first half of 1964.

The fact that Congress was not told of, and indeed was entirely misled about the nature of those operations, played a crucial part in manipulating Congress so as to get an appearance of support for a war about which, in fact, they had been grossly deceived.

So, again, it would have been better for all of us had Congress had the information which, in fact, Senator Morse appeared to have. But insofar as he alone was in possesion of it, he was not able to convince his fellow Senators.

The information about covert operations in Laos in the past and at present, information that Fred Branfman has brought to us, obviously is very long overdue. Finally, to get to the question of ongoing plans—ongoing operations—when will Congress decide that it has a need to know about the decision

[63]

making that went into the Cambodian invasion or the Laotian operation?

I put it as almost an exercise to people who have read these Papers, or to Congressmen who have access to the full set, that by careful study of the methods by which such decisions as the Tonkin Gulf Resolution go through, they can develop a set of good hypotheses about how they are being misled, abused and manipulated today as in past years.

They should be able to make some fairly accurate guesses as to what went on in the process leading up to our actions in Cambodia or Laos. There is no question that there was great deception in that process, and I think it is time for Congressmen to decide that they have a right to know and a need to know. Indeed, the public does deserve more than leaked stories to *Look Magazine* of classified information from within the administration.

They should have the memos, contingency plans and the estimates represented in the Pentagon Papers for those episodes. Finally, I think they should have some access, however limited, to the kinds of "contingency plans" that exist right now for the invasion and total bombing of North Vietnam.

MR. HALPERIN: Let me say, I have never been in Vietnam. I don't speak Vietnamese and I don't purport to be an expert on Vietnam or Vietnamese society. I think there are two different notions of what the first priority is regarding the war.

It is clear that Vietnam has raised a number of very fundamental issues about the role of the United States in the world, about the nature of our interests in the world, about the degree to which we can ignore the rights and interests of other people to insure what has to be done for our own security, the questions about the morality of the war, the questions about the decision-making structures, the powers of Congress and so on.

[64]

What has disturbed me is not what some of the discussion here has suggested, but some of the things that have been going on in Congress. We appear to be turning our attention to what would seem to be quite legitimate postwar issues and postwar problems before we are out of Indochina.

I think to say that we can't get out of Indochina until we reform our society is a prescription for a very lengthy United States presence in Indochina. While it may be true that the risk of further intervention will be great until there are fundamental changes in our society, it seems to me that we have to persevere in our attempts to get out of this war and then to stay out of any more wars, while at the same time doing what we can to improve our system.

But the notion that the Vietnam situation can only be resolved through a restructuring of our government or that it is more important for the Congress to worry about whether it should be notified thirty days or sixty days after we get into the next war, would be rather pointless in view of what seems to be the main issue now, which is, and I think we all agree, to get out of Indochina.

If we look at that question it becomes apparent that while there remain fundamental differences on all these other issues, if we at least examine the President's rhetoric, the issue has become quite narrowed down.

What the President says is that he is prepared for a total withdrawal when we can secure the release of our prisoners. It is now very clear that we can get our prisoners back any time we are prepared to set a date and get out.

So we have only the President's other stipulation, which is to assure a reasonable chance to the South Vietnamese to determine their own destiny. Now it isn't clear which South Vietnamese the President has in mind, or what his image is of what the sides are, if indeed there are sides in South Vietnam.

Nevertheless, it seems to me, if one allows for any reasonable interpretation of the notion of "reasonable chance," it becomes quite obvious that we have long since given much more than a reasonable chance to whatever elements there are in South Vietnam that wish to resist an NLF takeover, and that the time has therefore come to say to the administration, your stipulation has been met and it is time for a total United States withdrawal; that we can no longer hide behind the prisoner issue because it is now clear that we can get the prisoners back; and simply taking the President's own criteria, it is time to get out now.

I think the administration will, in fact, be prepared to set a deadline only if it becomes clear that the domestic pressure demands it, and domestic pressure demanding it simply means Congress voting to cut off the funds.

The Senate recently adopted the Mansfield amendment to the draft extension bill, which provides for a policy of withdrawal in nine months. I think the first priority is to convince Congress that the American people don't want the draft unless it also means an end to the war. (Whether or not they want it under other conditions is another question.) The second priority is to put teeth in the Mansfield amendment by voting to cut off funds for the war.

I think any Congressman or Senator who says Congress doesn't have the responsibility should be told very clearly that any Congressman or Senator who votes for funds to continue the war is assuming that responsibility and that it is time now to simply cut off the funds, hopefully with the President's support. But if not, he should be instructed to go ahead without the President's support and get United States forces out of Indochina and bring the American prisoners back.

Then, and only then, should we turn our attention to these other more fundamental issues, but issues which I think apply

right now to the basic question; that is, how do we get out of Indochina?

PROF. MIRSKY: We know from the Deputy Ambassador in Saigon that twenty thousand people have been assassinated in the Phoenix program, which is a CIA-inspired operation.

We know that there are millions of refugees in Indochina. We know that this country is illegally funding various sorts of military operations such as the use of Thai troops in Laos. We know from Fred Branfman that there are countless Lao people who are living under the ground week after week, and month after month, because they are afriad to come out to face the saturation bombing by United States planes.

We know that there are many students and others who have been imprisoned in Saigon for their political views. We know that there have been 350 thousand United States casualties and millions of Indochinese victims as well.

My sister-in-law at the Quaker hospital in Quang Ngai has reported to me over the last few months that as United States troops leave and the bombing increases, the number of civilian casualties with their arms and legs blown off is growing.

I agree with those who have stated that the war has to be stopped as a first condition. Following is a course of action I would urge every Congressman to pursue in order to bring the war to an end:

First, at every opportunity, whether in the well of the House or in any committee meeting, Congressmen should ask for time, even if it is only thirty seconds a day, to speak about the necessity to halt the war in Vietnam—that no day be missed should the opportunity arise.

Second, I would like to see a statement from members of Congress, fully supporting the acts of Daniel Ellsberg.

Third, I would like to see Congressmen supporting those

political prisoners now in Saigon; and specifically deploring the trial and capital charges of treason against leading Saigon students such as Huynh Tan Mam.

Fourth, I would like to see Congress institute legal proceedings against those in our administration who have provided funds and other aid for illegal acts such as those perpetrated in Laos. I refer, for instance, to Secretary Laird.

Fifth, I would like to see as many Congressmen as possible announce their support for the seven-point NFL peace proposal in Paris and demand that the Nixon administration, without delay, negotiate in Paris on the basis of this proposal.

And finally, I would like to see more members of Congress sign the Peoples' Peace Treaty.

PROF. GURTOV: I would like to address myself to the matter of illegal United States support of Thai and other intervention of nationals in Laos and Cambodia.

First of all, let me ask the rhetorical question: why is this point important? I think it is important because of the nature of the Nixon doctrine and because of what the Nixon doctrine and the Vietnamization program have meant for United States involvement in Indochina.

As has been pointed out, present United States strategy is essentially one of trading ground forces for air power. It also involves, as has been pointed out in the last two days, more extensive covert American involvement in the support, supplying and training of indigenous so-called anti-Communist forces in Cambodia and Laos, including financial assistance to Thai mercenaries.

It seems to me that if we are talking only about United States withdrawal from South Vietnam then we have to be aware, in fact we have to anticipate, the fact that there will be, even if we were able to bring this withdrawal about, a continuation and increase of the kinds of covert actions that we

now see taking place in Cambodia and Laos, just as the bombing is going to continue and increase.

Therefore, it seems to me, we should be very clear about the distinction between withdrawal from South Vietnam and termination of the United States role throughout Indochina. We should also be aware, again, of what the Nixon doctrine is going to mean for continued United States involvement outside Vietnam even if we were able to bring to an end the United States role in South Vietnam.

So, to come back to the beginning, it seems to me that we must do more than merely be attentive to the fact that the administration is violating the Fulbright Amendment. We should be aware that this sort of violation is going to continue in coming years unless the Congress acts to call the administration to account.

It is not calling the administration to account when, as in recent weeks and right down to July 28, some Senators point out in chambers that they believe the administration is violating the law.

For example, yesterday it was reported that Senator Case tried to present evidence to indicate that United States support of Thai mercenaries, in increasing numbers in Laos, was in violation of the law. The State and Defense Departments responded by claiming that we were not violating the Fulbright Amendment. After all, they said, these are only volunteers whom we are supporting. Of course, in a way this is a step forward, because in past years neither the administration nor the Royal Kingdom of Thailand would so much as admit that such volunteers were even present in Laos.

So we have made a small step forward. But the point is that this kind of action and other actions, such as the support for Thai air activity over Northeastern Cambodia, are in violation of the law.

The Congress or individual Congressmen ought to be prepared to institute a legal action against the Secretary of Defense in which they challenge the legality of the administration's right to support Thai mercenaries, under whatever label, in Cambodia and in Laos.

REP. DOW: I personally deplore our actions in Laos and Thailand. I have been to both these countries and I can't for the life of me understand why the United States is even remotely interested in Laos or where we envision any future for ourselves there.

It is, in every respect, a very fine country, but certainly it is no place for us. The fact that we ventured there, to my way of thinking, is an action that has been taken by the Executive which far exceeds its constitutional authority.

I think the sooner we get out of there the better. I do believe that we have been diverted by the main theme in Vietnam. If we have been a little heedless about what has happened in Laos and Cambodia and Thailand, it isn't because we are not concerned as you are, Professor Gurtov, but because the main theme in Vietnam has preoccupied us so deeply.

MR. RASKIN: I think it is useful to pick up on some of the points that Professor Halperin has made. Certainly I don't disagree with his view that as a first priority the United States must get out of Vietnam.

The problem, though, is that when we come to examine what that means, given the present institutional structure in the United States, we see that achieving such a priority is likely to precipitate a constitutional crisis.

For example, if it were the case that Congress voted against appropriations for the Indochina war or the United States presence in Indochina, thereby overriding a Presidential veto,

the hidden constitutional crisis which we are now living through would become apparent for all to see.

We should see a direct confrontation with the President's authority to assert foreign policy and make war on his own conditions. As you know, the Executive power of the government has well over two to three years of funds which it can call on to continue the war.

Both the increase in covert operations in Indochina as well as the hard facts of civilian control over the military would become manifest. Yet, it is necessary to run this "risk" if we are ever to get out of Indochina and begin the transformation of power within the country itself.

In all of this we should not fall into the trap of thinking that the Executive branch is the President: that he can wave a magic wand which could stop the war. The fact of the matter is that there are huge institutional strings which operate on him and through him which determine whether the war continues at one place or expands in another place or cause the confrontation.

While in one sense it may be correct rhetorically speaking, to argue for immediate withdrawal from Indochina, it is much more important, I think, for people to comprehend the implications of this undertaking; that is, it is not going to occur in a casual way. It will require a wholesale change of leadership as well as constitutional change. There is virtually no war in modern history where the losers have remained in power immediately after that loss. This war is no different. Thus, we must look to different groups to end the war.

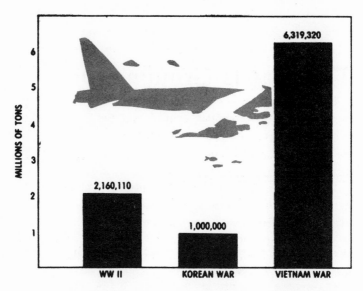

AIR MUNITIONS EXPENDED IN LAST THREE U.S. WARS

Reprinted from *The Impact of the Vietnam War*, by courtesy of Clergy and Laymen Concerned, 637 W. 125 St., N.Y., N.Y. 10027.

CHAPTER TWO

The War Is Grinding On

DR. GURTOV: Despite the best efforts of our government to make it appear otherwise, the Vietnam war remains the most urgent foreign-policy problem of the United States and the most corrosive influence on our domestic life. Thousands of lives—American, Vietnamese, Cambodian and Lao—are being lost every week in a war whose legitimacy few Americans now seem to uphold.

The times demand extraordinary action if the policies of the United States are to change and finally embrace termination of American involvement in Indochina as our overriding and essential objective. All of us should be grateful that a man has responded, at personal risk to his future freedom, in order that we be made more fully aware of the conditions surrounding our tragic involvement in Vietnam from 1945 to 1968.

The divulgence of the classified documents concerning United States decision making on the war, and the decision of the major newspapers to publish them, constitute a national service in the highest traditions of patriotism. The significance of the so-called Pentagon Papers goes well beyond history, for

these documents draw the attention of persons inside and outside the administration to the disturbing parallels between past and present. I refer not merely to the Nixon administration's pursuit of policies which, like those of preceding administrations, are in my judgment infeasible, unwise, and in some cases, immoral and reckless. Of greater concern to me is the continuation of a pattern of deception in American policy—deception of the Congress and the American people. The truth about United States objectives and activities in Indochina is being distorted or hidden as much now as before, a circumstance every bit as intolerable as the policies themselves.

The public record of the Nixon administration alone provides an adequate basis for reaching this conclusion. This record shows that like previous administrations:

1. This administration aims at achieving a military victory in Vietnam while professing to be striving for complete withdrawal. The gradual reductions of United States ground forces should not divert our attention from the expansion and intensification of our air power throughout Indochina, the creation of a new commitment to the survival of a non-Communist regime in Cambodia and the support, in contravention of the law (the Fulbright amendment), of South Vietnamese and Thai intervention in Laos.

2. This administration is not interested in negotiations to end United States involvement, except on terms that it knows North Vietnam cannot accept. Calls for mutual troop withdrawals and cease-fires are not meaningful bargaining terms; the administration surely knows in advance that such proposals, because of the conditions attached to them, will never be acceptable to the other side.

3. This administration, while paying lip service to self-determination in South Vietnam, continues to prop up a regime that is taking steps to prevent the holding of competitive

elections and the evolution of political accommodations among the contending Vietnamese factions.

4. This administration, while expressing concern for the safety and liberation of United States prisoners in North Vietnam, is in fact exploiting their captivity for domestic political purposes. The increasing number of POWs in North Vietnam's camps enables the administration to rationalize the long-term presence of United States forces in Indochina and the necessity to escalate the war in North Vietnam. The administration knows full well that the POWs will not be returned unless and until the United States sets a specific date for complete withdrawal from Vietnam.

5. This administration has willfully misled the American people into believing that its policies are consistently intended to extricate the United States from the war. It portrays escalation as de-escalation, and failure as success.

Intervention in Cambodia was not a response to a new threat from the sanctuaries, but was a United States-ARVN initiative to exploit the overthrow of Sihanouk.

The widespread use of air power in Cambodia is not designed to speed our troop withdrawals, but to support ARVN intervention and to sustain a militarily ineffective, unstable government.

"Protective reaction" strikes against North Vietnam are in fact attempts to punish Hanoi for continuing the war; they may also be warnings to Hanoi of United States willingness to revive the air war. Finally, the incursions into Laos did not demonstrate the ARVN's improvement, but showed, to the contrary, that "Vietnamization" cannot be carried out without heavy United States air and logistical support, and cannot succeed even with it.

6. This administration's "Vietnamization" policy is primarily a domestic political tactic, not a program for complete

withdrawal. Troop reductions are being geared to have maximum impact on our 1972 elections; they have far less to do with ARVN's performance.

Such reductions, moreover, are meant to distract attention from an unprecedented application of aerial destructiveness that promises not only increasing suffering for the people of the three countries, but also more American prisoners of war.

When a government consistently deceives its people about the purposes of its policies, it must be called to account. The leaders of previous administrations are now being judged by the people as the result of publication of the Pentagon Papers.

The fullest divulgence of the truth about present United States policies in Indochina can come about, however, only when the public and the Congress demand it.

The public must insist that their representatives press the administration to report on the extent and purpose of United States bombing in northern and southern Laos, as well as on the nature and objectives of United States support for South Vietnamese and Thai intervention in Laos and Cambodia.

The Congress should enact legislation to overhaul the system governing classified documents. Such legislation might establish a panel of individuals outside the government to monitor and recommend the rapid declassification of noncurrent materials; in addition, it might set up a system to assure automatic receipt of government studies by the relevant Congressional committees.

But the most urgent business of the American people and the Congress is to work for the removal of the United States from the war in Indochina. The administration must be persuaded to set a definite date for terminating United States involvement in return for the release of our prisoners and the unimpeded withdrawal of United States forces and bases from South Vietnam.

Such an arrangement is clearly obtainable. Public and Congressional pressure to secure it would constitute an appropriate and effective response to nearly twenty years of deceitful and fruitless government policy making on Indochina.

Ms. FREDRICK: Like many American citizens, I am deeply concerned about the extent to which the administration and the media have attempted to gloss over the real messages of the Pentagon Papers by focusing attention on issues only peripherally related to the central questions raised by the documents.

I believe these diversions reflect a conscious effort on the part of the administration and the media to save face, now that their past records have been exposed. I also believe—and I think this is even more serious—that these diversions are a deliberate attempt to ensure that we, the American public, will not see the critical link between the lies of the past and those of the present—and the future.

For twenty-five years, the United States government has not only been waging a war of destruction against the people of Indochina; through its influence over and manipulation of information related to United States policies and presence in Southeast Asia, it has also been waging a propaganda war against its own citizens.

This information war—reinforced by strong elements of racism within the United States—has led to the dehumanization of the people and the culture of Vietnam in the eyes of the American public. It has also thereby conditioned our attitudes about United States foreign policy.

We see no evidence at this time to suggest that the present administration has decided to change this policy of propagandizing the American people. Indeed, all evidence seems to point in the opposite direction. We might cite as two very

[77]

relevant examples the administration's current attempts to downplay and even ignore the significance of the PRG's 7-point peace proposal of July 1, 1971 and our government's efforts to hide from us the truth about the current political situation in Saigon.

United States involvement in Indochina, as the Pentagon Papers so clearly demonstrate, was neither accidental nor altruistic. On the contrary, American policy makers were the willing heirs to French colonial policy—a policy which depended on a program of "divide to rule" and of "Vietnamization" to impose and maintain influence over an unwilling people—a policy nowise different from that of the United States in Vietnam today.

The United States, unlike France, has not established an outright colonial regime in Saigon. Rather, it has attempted to rely on so-called "nationalist alternatives" as the most effective means of maintaining influence in that country—and has thereby ended up supporting the most unnationalistic regimes of all: Diem and Khanh in the 1950's and 1960's, Thieu-Ky-Khiem today—and tomorrow undoubtedly others of the same "nationalist" ilk, others like those who, during the Vietnamese war for independence from the French, fought on the side of the colonialists against their own Vietnamese brothers and sisters.

We see no evidence of any change in these policies under the present administration. Indeed, the basic assumptions which have determined United States policy in Indochina all these years seem today more clearly influential than ever.

Mr. Russo: When I was invited to participate in this conference, I hesitated because I am currently involved in litigation concerning the Pentagon Papers. I have been sentenced to jail for refusing to testify before a grand jury. But after giv-

ing the matter some thought, I agreed to participate because I think that one of the most important issues has been totally overlooked by the Pentagon Papers.

It has become apparent that the Pentagon Papers do not address themselves to the Vietnamese people. In this war, in addition to the deaths of forty-five thousand Americans, the many thousands more who are maimed, who have returned without legs, arms or eyes, who are addicted to heroin—in addition to all this, my studies of the war indicate that by very conservative estimates the United States has been responsible for the deaths of between 500 thousand and one million Vietnamese. This statistic does not of course take into account the countless numbers of Vietnamese who have been mutilated and whose lives have been effectively destroyed.

Virtually half the country has been driven to take refuge, a situation which I would think points up the fact that the United States has learned nothing from World War II.

In Vietnam we have conducted a genocidal war which has resulted in the depersonalization of the Vietnamese people. I think that this is perhaps the greatest sin of all.

The United States has always ignored the problems and the realities of Vietnam, as it is now ignoring the problems and realities of its own situation at home.

Vietnam to me is a reflection of that part of the American character which promotes social injustice in its own backyard. Moreover, it is my belief that present policy with regard to Vietnam rests on as many lies and as much deceit as is revealed in the Pentagon Papers. Vietnamization, for example, is in my opinion one of the most misleading concepts that the present administration has proposed.

The Vietnamese Army, that is, the Saigon Army, seems to be in very much the same shape today as it was as long ago as 1954. The Americans were then proclaiming that if given a

little more time they would be able to get things in shape, they would have the Air Force ready and, in just another year, they would be organized. That was seventeen years ago, and the Saigon Army is still not an effective force.

I think a great deal depends, in this situation, on motivation. The Saigon Army, that is, the elite of the Army, has no motivation other than to feather its own nest. Herein lies the entire question of Vietnamization, which, as I have already stated, is a blatant set of lies and deception.

My feeling is that our POW situation in North Vietnam is similarly misleading. I am as concerned as anyone else for Americans who have been held captive by the North Vietnamese. However, to make them pawns in this situation, I think, is the ultimate in hypocrisy.

The eighteen months I spent in Vietnam interviewing Viet Cong prisoners in the jails of South Vietnam taught me a great deal. The United States makes demands for lists and asks for all of the information about the prisoners who are held in North Vietnam. However, even at the jails in South Vietnam, the jail keeper does not have a list of the names of the people who are being held there. This was when I learned that the prisoners were treated most inhumanely, that in fact they were subjected to torture, and, at times, they were summarily executed.

My observations have led me to believe that United States involvement in Vietnam has been disastrous on all counts—politically, socially and economically. The United States has won for itself the world image of absolutist bully.

In order to deny the Viet Cong support—it having become apparent that they could be fought in no other way—the United States had to resort to a destruction of the very environment within which the people lived. By so doing, the United States has opened itself up to charges of genocide and imperialism.

[80]

If I remember correctly, *The Encyclopedia Brittanica* defines imperialism as the controlling by one country of a people outside its own borders. I do not think that anybody can deny that this is precisely what the United States has attempted to do.

The determination of the Executive branch, through a number of administrations, to pursue, and even escalate, an undeclared war has set the United States on a course toward absolutism. Consequently both her domestic unity and her foreign policy consensus have begun to crumble—and American youth are rebelling.

DR. GURTOV: I would say that the present administration has learned one thing from all these years of United States involvement. It has learned how to pursue the very objectives pursued by previous administrations by packaging them more skillfully. The administration clearly recognizes the importance of domestic public opinion. "Vietnamization" is a classic example of this new kind of sales pitch. "Vietnamization" permits the administration to pursue the same goal as before, i.e., that of preserving a non-Communist independent Vietnam, free from "external" influence.

The substitution of air power for United States ground power in order to reduce American casualties is another example of packaging. Of course, it is the hope of the administration that fewer American casualties will satisfy the American people, who will then ignore the fact that an increasing number of Vietnamese, Cambodians and Laotians are being killed, maimed, or left homeless.

Yet another example of this kind of packaging is the response of the United States government to the peace proposal in Paris. It is interesting that after so many months of many hints about what the other side would give in return for our

setting a firm timetable for withdrawal, the NLF and the North Vietnamese came out with a very clear statement, which indicated that in fact the trade-off would be prisoners for a timetable.

The administration was deeply embarrassed by this proposal and chose to respond by refusing to consider the points to be bargained for: it was determined not to open serious negotiations with the other side.

The question asked was: how do we package our rejection? And the way the administration packaged it was by first having the State Department say that while the proposal was interesting, it was very complex and contained a number of ambiguities. Finally, the order was given to Ambassador Bruce in Paris that he should pursue the matter with the other side, but, of course, in secret, so that our refusal would not become public and, therefore, an embarrassment.

Utilizing these and other tactics, the administration is showing us that through the Vietnam experience, it is learning how to manipulate public opinion, the press and the Congress in ways more sophisticated than those of previous administrations.

MR. RUSSO: The effect of the publication of the Pentagon Papers is that it has opened the eyes of the American public. I agree with Dr. Gurtov in that I think it has had no effect on the Nixon administration, except for indicating the need to sharpen up its public relations.

By this I mean that the administration has not changed. I think its policies are still based on lies and deception, and that it is probably looking for ways to become even more deceptive.

MR. BRANFMAN: I would like to speak briefly about what has

gone on since the Nixon administration took office. At the beginning of this administration, the bombing in North Vietnam had stopped, Cambodia was in peace and the bombing of Laos was relatively moderate.

Subsequently, however, we have invaded Cambodia and engaged in massive bombings of that country. We have doubled the bombing of Laos and resumed the bombing of North Vietnam, twice a week since the first of the year.

More relevant, I think, what struck me most on my return from Laos is that while we are de-escalating in terms of manpower in Vietnam, we are actually building up United States manpower in Laos. There are more Americans directing military operations in Laos, and over a million dollars have gone for American personnel in the last year.

Indeed, since the publication of The Pentagon Papers, Cambodia has been invaded, and a military offensive has been mounted against the Plain of Jars. I think this course of action is sufficient proof that the war is not winding down. It having become apparent that the Pentagon Papers have had very little effect on the Executive determination to continue the war, it is only natural that we should turn our attention to the system and the way it works. I think the problem lies in the system. Since the end of World War II there has been a proliferation of technology, which by its nature means more and more power for destruction. The Executive branch has increasingly been in control of the use of this power. We can hardly look to Congress to curtail this Executive control because I think most Congressmen basically agree with what is going on, and those who do not are often silent.

Something, however, can be done. I propose that those Congressmen who do oppose the war, but who do not have the knowledge and do not have the facts, should make this withholding of facts clear to the American public. This is espe-

cially important in that we are now engaged in an automated air war about which there is almost no public information.

MR. LUCE: I don't think the war is winding down at all. I think the tactics are merely changing in that we have shifted from a ground-troop war to an air war. Certainly if you are a villager in Vietnam you are hardly comforted by the fact that your village is now being bombed instead of attacked from the ground. More people are killed from bombing than when troops attack a village from the ground.

Another change in tactics involves American economic aid. Last year, for example, we gave some twenty-one million dollars to the Saigon police force. This year we have increased the amount to thirty million dollars.

Last year we gave 6.1 million dollars to the education system. This year we have decreased this contribution to four-and-a-half million dollars. We are now spending more than six times as much on police work as we are on the whole education system. In terms of our economic aid, we are placing more and more emphasis on military power.

I also think that one of the things we sometimes forget—in talking about the rules of war and constitutional law, and the like—is that not only do secret documents like the Pentagon Papers indicate that our government advocates and condones the violations, but also, that our very top government officials are doing this publicly.

I refer you, for example, to a May 3, 1970, ''Face the Nation'' speech of Vice President Spiro Agnew in which he said that our purpose for going in and bombing was, among other things, to destroy a hospital complex. This is in direct violation of Article Nineteen of the Geneva Convention on the treatment of the war wounded. That such acts are condoned so

openly, I believe, has passed without any notice here in the United States.

PROF. MIRSKY: We stand now, in my judgment, at a pivotal point. There are very few choices that remain for the policy makers of the United States. We can get out of Indochina forthwith; we can further escalate from Cambodia to Laos to North Vietnam; we can employ nuclear weapons; and it is still possible that we can directly challenge Peking.

Suppose we choose not to leave the Indochina scene at once. Why do I believe that escalation is the inevitable course? Let us examine the case of Laos. Why was this operation guaranteed to fail?

The entire invasion route was heavily fortified by the North Vietnamese who smashed the ARVN on the ground and shot more than 250 United States helicopters from the sky. We know from CIA reports that thirty thousand Viet Cong had infiltrated the Saigon government to the highest levels, so it comes as no surprise that some kind of advance preparations were made.

The military failure in Laos can not, of course, alter the situation in that kingdom which is already half dominated by the Pathet Lao. It can only weaken yet further the standing of the unsteady so-called "neutralist" Lao regime which explicitly asked the United States not to invade.

Nor has the Laos defeat done anything to strengthen Washington's allies in Cambodia, for since the 1969 May invasion, most of that country has fallen under the control of our adversaries.

In both Laos and Cambodia, as in South Vietnam—and this is the central point that I want to make—the populations tend to support our opponents because they protect the local people from United States military operations. "Our" Indochinese

desert because they view themselves as fighting for foreigners, while by now our opponents are widely regarded as patriots.

Can we again call upon the shattered ARVN to do our dying for us? Is this Vietnamization? Shall we kill five or six thousand more ARVN troops to save American lives? In the words of Ambassador Bunker, did we only change the color of the corpses by invading two countries, and bombing three, to protect our President's credibility in a fourth?

The President is now facing a crisis. His conventional military means have proven ineffective. (The word "conventional," of course, is used only in the American sense.) The ARVN won't fight and may mutiny.

Last year United States soldiers, reluctant to fight an ambiguous war, turned increasingly to drugs, refused orders, and even killed scores of their officers.

Shall we then, unable to achieve an end that we should never have desired, destroy the ancient cultures and peoples of Indochina because we cannot win their hearts and minds? Are their bodies so cheap?

The Senate Subcommittee on Refugees has recently stated: "In this year, 1971, more civilians are being killed and wounded in the three countries of Indochina and many more made refugees that at any time in history. Most of the casualties are caused, and people made refugees, by American and allied military activities."

Such melancholy assessments must cast doubt on the assertion that "the war is winding down," which is the present big lie. Four million South Vietnamese, one million Cambodians, and at least 600 thousand Lao are refugees, the survivors of the more than one million civilians killed by our bombing, our harassment and interdiction, our Phoenix assassination program which has claimed 20 thousand lives, and our search-

and-destroy policy. These casualties all bear witness to the failure of our vision and our intention in Indochina.

They exceed in number, but not in value, the fifty thousand dead and 300,000 wounded Americans. Hence, the big question is: Why have we allowed this to happen? I think it is because we have two standards of morality—one for ourselves here at home and another for those in distant lands.

We normally won't stand for murder, torture and assault at home. We feel that inside ourselves, although we also know that many of us are potentially murderers, torturers and assaulters.

But, because we are potential murderers, torturers and assaulters, we are willing to entrust such acts to others at a distance. As long as the policy makers are willing to cloak our murder and torture in terms such as "national defense," "patriotism," "obligation" and even "responsibility," we allow the flow of blood to continue. We all know what is happening, and at the same time, we know that it is wrong.

The conflict created by these two standards is tearing apart the decent people of this country. In an address at Dartmouth, General Telford Taylor, one of the prosecutors at Nuremburg, after admitting that war crimes are being committed and that high officials may be responsible, warned the Dartmouth audience that our body politic can not tolerate an investigation of the origins of American bestiality in Southeast Asia.

I think, on the contrary, that it must be subjected to such an investigation. When we face what we are, what apparently we sometimes enjoy doing, what we hide by letting others do it, we will be taking a step toward sanity. Such an analysis will be agonizing for all of us, but without it, the numbness which we can all feel as it creeps inside us, will reach our hearts.

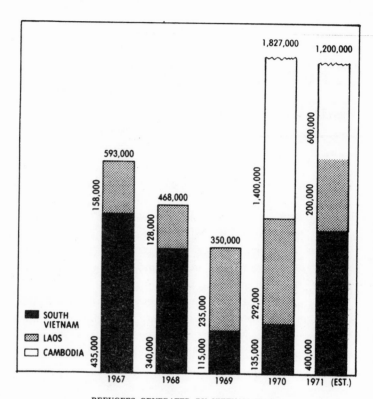

REFUGEES GENERATED BY VIETNAM WAR

Reprinted from *The Impact of the Vietnam War,* by courtesy of Clergy and Laymen
Concerned, 637 W. 125 St., N.Y., N.Y. 10027.

[88]

CHAPTER THREE

"The Southern Duck
Wants to Lie Down"

PROF. DINH: I would like to address myself to six major questions with which this conference is concerned.

The first one asks, "what were the critical turning points in United States involvement in Vietnam and how were they handled?" I would answer as follows:

1. May 10, 1854—when a detachment of United States Marines under the command of Captain John (Mad Jack) Percival, landed in Da Nang and forced the Vietnamese Emperor to release a French Bishop. That was the first United States interference in Vietnamese affairs on the side of the French.

2. September 2, 1945—when President Ho Chi Minh proclaimed, in Hanoi, the independence of Vietnam. The United States should have recognized the government of the Democratic Republic of Vietnam under Ho Chi Minh. It did not.

3. May 8, 1950—when the United States, after having recognized the French-sponsored Bao Dai government (February 7, 1950), announced that it would provide economic and military aid to the French in Indochina. In 1950 the French started "Vietnamizing" the war which ended in the French defeat at Dien Bien Phu. The United States aid program ulti-

mately reached $1.1 billion, paying 78 per cent of the French war burden.

4. July 1956—when elections for the reunification of Vietnam should have taken place under the supervision of the International Control Commission, in accordance with the 1954 Geneva Agreements (Article 7 of the Final Declaration of the Geneva Conference, July 21, 1954). They did not take place.

5. November 1, 1963—when the Ngo Dinh Diem regime was overthrown in a *coup d'état.* The United States should have withdrawn its commitments then, and, of course, it should not have participated in the planning of the coup.

6. July 1, 1971—when the Provisional Revolutionary Government of South Vietnam proposed at the Paris talks a seven-point program for the withdrawal of United States troops and the release of all military men of all parties and civilians captured during the war, including United States pilots taken prisoner in North Vietnam. We have already heard, at this Conference, the United States response.

The second question deals with the United States Constitution and whether it was ignored and violated throughout the course of United States involvement in Southeast Asia. Because I am not a United States citizen, I refrain from answering this question. The fact that the United States has interfered in the affairs of the Vietnamese does not give me permission to retaliate by interfering in the internal political affairs of this country.

For this same reason I will not address myself to the question of whether or not past and present United States Presidents and Congresses have failed to function properly.

I can not speak about the effect of the publication of the Pentagon Papers on the Nixon administration policy. I can speak only about the effects of the Pentagon Papers on the Vietnamese. The Papers confirm what many Vietnamese had

long been suspecting: the United States has not respected the principle of self-determination. The people who have made decisions which affected the life and death of the Vietnamese have shown a majestic contempt for the Vietnamese people and their history, the main characteristic of which has been a persistent, heroic resistance against all foreign domination no matter by whom—Han Chinese, Mongolians, Manchus, French or Japanese. The contempt for South Vietnamese generals for whom Americans were sent to die is clear from the account of General Taylor's meeting with members of the Saigon military junta, December, 1964. [1] General Taylor extended the same contempt to the leaders of North Vietnam. In an interview published in *The Washington Sunday Evening Star*, July 18, 1971, he had this to say: "I was simply amazed that North Vietnam would come out and attack our Navy on the high seas and that worried me. It always worries me when I find an opponent doing something that you wonder maybe he'll do something else so unexpectedly stupid that he'll completely upset the applecart." Well, General Taylor should have been better informed about the details of the so-called Gulf of Tonkin incident. Also one can say anything one likes about the leaders of North Vietnam but one can not call them stupid. The whole world, and certainly the Vietnamese people, know they are not. Besides, General Taylor doesn't need to worry, now that he is back safely in this country.

The next question asked: "What assumptions of United States foreign policy of the past twenty-five years have been called into question as a result of the material contained within the documents?" I would answer that as follows:

1. That because the leadership of the August 1945 revolu-

[1] *The Pentagon Papers*, as published by *The New York Times*, New York: Bantam, 1971, Document 89, p. 379.

tion in Vietnam was Communist, Vietnam would become a colony of the USSR or a Manchukuo of China.

2. That Vietnam has never been a nation, and that the Vietnamese, with a history of three thousand years, need the two-hundred year-old United States to build a nation for them. Perhaps it is useful for those who are still in doubt about Vietnamese nationalism to read here the translation of a short poem composed by Ly Thuong Kiet, a commander of the Vietnamese army, who from 1075 to 1077 opposed with success the repeated attacks launched on Vietnamese by the Chinese Sung:

The Emperors of the South rule over the rivers and the mountains of the Southern Country,
This destiny has been registered indelibly in the Celestial Book
How dare you, rebellious slaves come violate it?
You shall undoubtedly witness your own complete defeat.

That was written in the eleventh century. It is still true today and will be true tomorrow.

3. That the peasants want to be left alone and do not care about politics. The peasants of Vietnam, through sweat, blood, tears and community actions, are the most sophisticated elements in the society. They are the real heroes in the long history of Vietnam, and they are the most beautiful human beings.

And finally is the question of what should be the course of United States withdrawal from Southeast Asia. I leave this question to others. I can speak neither as an American nor as a representative of the peoples of Southeast Asia. One thing I can say is that I hope the Congress will set a date for the United States to withdraw "lock, stock and barrel" from Vietnam and then leave all the problems of Vietnam for the Viet-

namese to settle among themselves. In other words, the United States should accept the 7-point program proposed by the Provisional Revolutionary Government.

PROF. MARR: In the next decade or so, there are bound to be scores of books and hundreds of learned discussions of the Pentagon Papers. Many of us will be involved in that longer-term process of analysis, comparison and reconsideration. At this point, however, I would like to advance only a few points that interest me most, based on my experiences in the study of Vietnam over the past ten years.

Perhaps the most striking revelation for me in the Pentagon Papers was the consistent shallowness, the intellectual vacuity running through the policy documents of each administration, from Truman's onward. There was little, if any, patient, sustained discussion of broad policy options beyond the immediate "party line." There was absolutely no serious review of the philosophical or moral premises or postulates underlying policy. In short, some sort of selection process made certain that there were hundreds of people good at cranking out neat little "position papers," "memos," and "contingency plans," but nobody who knew, or could define for others, what it all meant.

I think the primary cause was ideological dogmatism, something we are always ready to charge Communist planners with, but seldom admit to among ourselves.

The underlying postulates were not discussed simply because they were taken for granted. With certain *a priori* beliefs dominating policy execution and response in this fashion, it must have been very difficult for ideas and data that countered those beliefs to gain a serious hearing.

The best example, in my opinion, was the steadfast belief that there existed an international Soviet-Chinese-DRV-NLF

conspiracy not only to unite Vietnam, but to seize all of Southeast Asia and the world.

For some reason, Vietnam was also conceived to be at the focal point of all this plotting, and if Vietnam fell, so too would all other countries elsewhere—at least as far away as Latin America and Africa.

With such an outlook, it was no problem for these men to argue that the DRV was perpetrating "aggression" against South Vietnam, or even that the NLF was committing "internal" aggression against its own brothers and sisters.

Of course, we heard all these arguments in public statements. It came nevertheless as something of a surprise for me to read the classified documents which forced me to conclude that these politicians and administrators really believed the shallow rhetoric they were passing out for public consumption.

It is often stated that United States policy makers should have read more Vietnamese history before committing themselves so deeply in that country. In point of fact, however, the Pentagon Papers show us that it would not have done any good.

Inasmuch as all the policy makers were sure that Communism had to be stood down in Vietnam, regardless of local conditions, they hardly felt the need to study local conditions. A Red was a bloody Red, no matter where you fought him.

This ignorance of modern Vietnamese history, however, led to some very significant miscalculations. A 1952 National Security Council policy paper,[2] for example, spoke of helping the French oppose the "Viet Minh rebellion," totally ignoring the fact that most Vietnamese believed the Viet Minh, as of 1945, to be the legitimate national leadership of their country.

This same sort of ideological blindness led to the formulators of a 1961 "action program" to advocate dropping leaflets over

[2] Ibid., pp. 29–31.

the DRV in order to "maintain morale of (the) North Vietnamese population." [3]

There was also a very naïve belief about how much our vaunted United States "counterinsurgency" specialists would be able to teach their Vietnamese followers when engaging in struggle with the Viet Minh, and later the NLF. Once again this stemmed from the presumption that American anti-Communist experiences in one part of the world could simply be transposed to Vietnam.

As it happened, however, even a legendary expert like Colonel Lansdale [4] turned out to be a mere babe-in-the-woods in Vietnam, in comparison with a middle-level Viet Minh cadre.

A far more tragic, deadly mistake growing out of historical ignorance, however, was to believe, in 1964–1965, that massive retaliation against the DRV, or even the threat of such retaliation, would be enough to halt or contain the struggle in South Vietnam. First of all, it was a misreading of the subtle relationship between the DRV and the NLF. Secondly, and much more significantly, it represented a total misunderstanding of how committed, emotionally and psychologically, both the DRV and the NLF were to what they considered a century-long struggle to eliminate imperialism from their country.

It was this lack of comprehension that led Henry Cabot Lodge (from October–November, 1963) to seriously advocate a Pavlovian carrot-and-stick approach, wherein the United States secretly offered North Vietnam economic aid in return for "calling off" the Viet Cong. If they would not be bought off, then they should be blasted from the air until they learned to salivate properly. Rostow operated from similar premises

[3] Ibid., p. 91.
[4] Ibid., pp. 633–634.

when he argued that a credible threat to DRV industry would be enough to halt the Viet Cong.

The Joint Chiefs of Staff planned to demand that the DRV conduct all their communications on the networks out of the north entirely in uncoded form, surely one of the better examples of modern neocolonial arrogance. Nobody seemed to sense that thousands of men and women who had spent ten, twenty, thirty years in protracted struggle—most of the time under even more desperate circumstances—were not about to cave in and prostrate themselves before the almighty American god of jet engines and electrons.

As we all know, by May or June of 1965, it was apparent that the enemy was not responding to Pavlovian treatment. This led us inevitably, given ideological presuppositions, to commit hundreds of thousands of ground troops.

In conclusion, I would like to point out the demeaning arrogance toward the Vietnamese people in general, and our Vietnamese associates in particular, that permeates the documents. Mostly it is expressed by simply ignoring them. Occasionally it comes out as adolescent petulance, as, for example, when Ambassador Durbrow (in September, 1960) snaps that President Diem had better shape up or be shipped out. Or there is the time when Ambassador Taylor (December, 1964) dresses down Generals Ky, Thieu, and Thi as though they were little children. And on the eve of the November, 1963 coup to overthrow Diem, Ambassador Lodge justifies all his complicity by saying that the "U.S. is trying to bring this medieval country into the twentieth century."

Even more self-defeating than any of these attitudes, nevertheless, is the idea that the Vietnamese peasantry is mere putty in the hands of anyone who stands over it with a gun. As Taylor phrases this primary American assumption (August, 1964):

Population support in the countryside is directly proportionate to the degree of GVN protection. There are grounds to conclude that no sophisticated approach is necessary to attract the country people to the GVN at this time. The assurance of a reasonably secure life is all that is necessary. [5]

When this sort of facile, essentially racist thinking proved erroneous, we certainly did not reconsider our basic commitment. If extending "security" to the peasants was not enough to induce them to avoid the NLF, why then, we would forcefully bring the peasants to security—by bombing, defoliating, and shipping them into refugee camps.

Now that it is apparent that even such Draconian, even genocidal measures have failed to bring the Vietnamese around to our way of thinking, I see no concrete evidence that the Nixon administration has re-examined the situation in fundamental fashion, down to, and including, the ideological premises.

I believe our primary effort here at this conference should be to map out the re-examination that should take place in light of the Pentagon Papers, and then press for an immediate, high-priority, public effort along those lines.

MR. LONG: I would like to make two points concerning the Pentagon Papers.

First, the Pentagon Papers show that none of these people, neither the American policy makers nor the Pentagon historians, knows anything about, or pays any attention to, the history of Vietnam. Nowhere in the Pentagon Papers can one find any reference to the French colonial period. Nor is there any mention of how the French colonizers had subverted the entire social, economic and political order of Vietnam.

[5] Ibid., p. 293.

There is no awareness that economically, for example, due to the French "land expropriation and free land concession policy," more than two-fifths of the cultivated surface in Vietnam passed into the hands of Frenchmen and Vietnamese collaborators, leaving the majority of the Vietnamese peasants without any land of their own. Because there were no significant industrial or commercial activities, these landless peasants had to become tenant farmers and sharecroppers, paying to their landlords basic rents of at least fifty per cent of their crops as well as all production costs.

This together with the fact that because farming was not mechanized, the maximum amount of land that a peasant could realistically work on was only about three acres, meant that the peasants throughout Vietnam had to live in constant hunger all through the French colonial period.

Meanwhile, every year the French exported an average of about two million metric tons of rice, or enough to feed ten million persons a year with 440 pounds per capita. Because there was always an insufficient supply of rice remaining for consumption within the country, every natural calamity resulted in mass starvation.

The worst period of starvation occurred late in 1944 and early in 1945 as a result of a rice collection policy initiated by the French and the Japanese. The conditions at this time inspired the following passage in the report of a certain French colonial officer by the name of Vespy: [6]

They walk in unending lines together with their whole families. There are old people and there are children; there are men and women, shrunken under the weight of their poverty and suffering.

[6] For the complete report, see *Témoignages et Documents Français Relatifs à la Colonization Française au Vietnam.* Hanoi: Association Culturelle pour le Salut du Vietnam, 1945, pp. 10–15.

Their bodies are nearly or all naked and the bones jut out, shaking . . . Now and again they stop to close the eyes of those who fall never to rise again, or to strip off any pieces of rag (I do not know what to call it exactly) which are left behind on their bodies. From looking at these bodies, which are more ugly than the ugliest of animals, and at these corpses, which are shrivelled up on the roadsides with only a handful of straw for clothes as well as for their burial garment, one feels ashamed of being a human.

It was precisely during this period that the Vietnamese people all over the country came together under the leadership of the Viet Minh, short for "League for the Independence of Vietnam," in an attempt to rid the country of the French and the Japanese.

But nowhere in the Pentagon Papers can one find a discussion of the Viet Minh, what they did for the people of Vietnam and how they gained the support of the people of that country.

The only comment on the Viet Minh was made by the Lansdale team in their report in 1955, which reads as follows: "The Viet Minh long ago had adopted the Chinese Communist thought that the people are the water and the army is the fish." [7]

What was never explained, however, was what type of fish in what kind of water. And it is obvious that the American policy makers never bothered to find out. To them the Viet Minh does not exist. It is seen as a communist movement, just as simply as that, and as such, it must be destroyed.

Such was the thinking behind the decision to support the French in their attempt to reconquer Vietnam and the decision to sabotage the Geneva Conference. When this was not successful, a decision was made to maintain an independent,

[7] *The Pentagon Papers*, op. cit., p. 63.

non-Communist and pro-United States South Vietnam, contrary to the stipulation of the Geneva Agreements that general elections were to be held by 1956 to assure the unification of the whole country under the supervision of an international commission.

To maintain an independent, non-Communist, pro-United States South Vietnam, the United States has sought to make the Saigon regime "effective" by maintaining the former French collaborators and the colonial status quo; by building up the defeated mercenary Saigon force of no more than fifty thousand men to over a million men; and by pacifying the countryside through massive relocation programs such as the "qui khu-qui ap," the "agrovilles," the strategic hamlets, not to mention the anticrop chemicals and gases, bombs and artillery strikes which the military regards as effective means for "urbanizing" the rural population, or "drying up the ocean."

"Effectiveness" is the one word that appears over and over and over again in the Pentagon documents. The assumption has been that if somehow the United States could make the Saigon regime effective, the people of Vietnam will support it.

It apparently never enters the minds of the American policy makers that for most Vietnamese it is simply not enough just to rid the country of the French colonizers if the social ills created during that occupation are allowed to continue.

The more a Saigon regime tries to be "effective," at the prodding of the United States, the more it gets into trouble. Thus when the Diem regime met with difficulties in its attempts to be effective, individual leaders were blamed for not understanding Western concepts, for refusing to widen the base of their government according to parliamentary process, democracy and so forth, and were subsequently deposed.

The most fantastic and most persistent misconception of all is that there is no such thing as Vietnamese nationalism. Fol-

lowing is a quote from General Taylor's briefing of key officials in November, 1964.

> As the past history of this country shows, there seems to be a national attribute which makes for factionalism and limits the development of a truly national spirit. Whether this tendency is innate or a development growing out of the conditions of political suppression under which successive generations have lived is hard to determine.

In the very next paragraph of the same report, however, General Taylor has this to say:

> The ability of the Viet Cong continuously to rebuild their units and to make good their losses is one of the mysteries of this guerilla war. We are aware of the recruiting methods by which local boys are induced or compelled to join the Viet Cong ranks and have some general appreciation of the amount of infiltration of personnel from the outside. Yet taking both these sources into account, we still find no plausible explanation of the continued strength of the Viet Cong if our data on Viet Cong losses are even approximately correct. Not only do the Viet Cong units have the recuperative powers of the phoenix, but they have an amazing ability to maintain morale. Only in rare cases have we found evidences of bad morale among Viet Cong prisoners or recorded in captured Viet Cong documents. [8]

The American policy makers simply refuse to understand the most obvious. Just as in the case of the Viet Minh, the Viet Cong is denied any nationalistic tendency. To the American policy makers the Viet Cong does not count; it is simply a "political arm" of the Communists. For this reason, the northern part of Vietnam had to be bombed (according to most of the policy makers) or bought off (in the view of Assistant Secretary of Defense McNaughton) with the promise that the

[8] Ibid., pp. 371–372.

[101]

United States would "arrange a rice-barter deal between two halves of Vietnam."

There is no appreciation of the fact that the problem in Vietnam is not rice but the equalization of national resources and the ridding it of foreigners.

My second point is that no attention is ever given to human suffering in the Pentagon Papers, with the possible exception of a statement by McNaughton in 1964 and 1965: "To emerge from crisis without unacceptable taint from methods used." [9]

In light of all the horrible methods used in Vietnam on the part of the United States since 1954, this total disregard for humanity is incredible. For without knowing what the reactions of the Vietnamese people are to the suffering imposed upon them by the United States, the United States has gone deeper and deeper into the morass of war.

MR. LUCE: When one talks about the suffering of the Vietnamese people, something should be said about the refugee problem. I worked with refugee camps, particularly from 1964 and 1965 up until I left Vietnam in May of 1971. The refugee problem is a very tragic thing.

What has happened is that the men have usually gone into one army or another. The women and children have been crowded around the air bases and into the city slums. They live in rooms perhaps ten feet square, with twelve or thirteen people in a room. Their diet is inadequate. The disease rate is extremely high.

The last figures I saw from the World Health Organization indicated that Vietnam had the highest rate of plague of any country in the world. The use of morphine and other drugs has risen steadily in these slum areas. We are destroying people who have been urbanized.

[9] Ibid., pp. 365, 432.

MR. TRUONG: I think the Pentagon Papers reflect the fact that for the United States, the only Vietnamese who seem to exist are the current leaders in Saigon, or previous members of military juntas, and President Diem.

I think that people in the United States, especially members of Congress should pay more attention to what the Vietnamese in general say.

If one gimmick does not work, then another is tried. A case in point at the present time is Operation Phoenix, which seems to be generating an increasing number of prisoners in South Vietnam's jails, while American companies are building more and more tiger cages and prison facilities.

I am glad to note that because of the publication of the Pentagon Papers, we have been able to assemble here to discuss and to see what we can do, by sharing our views, to bring an end to this conflict.

I think, as Dr. Daniel Ellsberg has stated repeatedly on television and on radio, that one should not lose sight of the fact that the content of the Pentagon Papers should not just be the center of academic discussions and debate, but that these discussions should provide the basis for further political action either by Congress or by the Executive branch (if it ever comes around to finding a political consensus) that could provide the people of South Vietnam and of North Vietnam with a settlement which would reflect their aspirations.

I have not come here to speak as a representative of any Vietnamese group, or for anybody else but myself. I think it is time for most of us, Vietnamese included, to try to increase the cooperation and at least open channels of communication, not with just the Vietnamese in power—like General Thieu— or generals involved in drug traffic, but with Vietnamese personalities, either in the opposition or within the Saigon regime. And through this increased cooperation, exert enough

pressure and political action by perhaps setting a date for voting on a resolution for a commitment to a specific deadline for the withdrawal of all United States troops. We should aim to get President Nixon to allow—perhaps for the first time in some thirty years—the people of South Vietnam to hammer out their own political settlement and chart their own political future.

GEN. THI: The Pentagon Papers reinforce and confirm the belief of my countrymen that the worsening condition in Vietnam has been caused by the interference of foreigners who did not understand the nature of the war and the culture of my country.

The heavy United States involvement was due to the desire of successive American administrations to create and support weak and corrupt Saigon governments loyal only to ambassadors and advisors of the United States.

The Vietnamese people in the South do not like to live under Communism, but we certainly do not want to fight proletarian dictators only to get military dictators under the protection of foreign military power.

United States policy makers have underestimated the nationalist sentiment and strength of the Vietnamese people. That is the main reason for the failure in Vietnam.

We Vietnamese understand that the American people want to help us, and we are deeply grateful for that; but unsound policies have caused more harm than help to my people and devastating destruction to my country.

The culture in South Vietnam has degenerated. Many of your soldiers and my people have been saturated with drugs because of war profiteers in top government positions in Saigon.

It is time to stop this tragic error from exhausting your tax-

payers' money, from dividing your people and from killing more Vietnamese and American youth.

While the withdrawal rate of United States troops should be accelerated, the bombing and shelling of villages, the intimidation and assassination of villagers in the Phoenix program should be stopped immediately.

REP. RYAN: I know that several participants of this conference have said that the Pentagon Papers reveal an incredible failure on the part of the United States to understand or appreciate Vietnamese history, a failure to understand nationalism in Southeast Asia, and a determination to maintain in power a so-called independent non-Communist South Vietnamese government.

My questions are: Do we now better understand the aspirations for nationalism in Vietnam? Is it our policy still to maintain and prop up a non-Communist, United States-controlled South Vietnamese government, regardless of what the will of the people may be? These are questions we ought to discuss throughout these proceedings.

MR. LONG: Representative Ryan, it seems to me that at the present time there is a misunderstanding. As an example of that, the President sent Mr. Kissinger and a lot of people scurrying around the world, looking for peace—trying to pressure the Chinese, or trying to get the Chinese to pressure the Vietnamese people in terms of a favorable way out for the United States. But Nixon is not going to find a solution in Peking, or anywhere else outside of Vietnam.

The real problem is the Vietnamese people mobilized against the United States, and American leaders simply refuse to recognize this. Not until American policymakers recognize that "the enemy" is the Vietnamese people, all these people the

United States has been bombing all this time, will there possibly be a way to get out of Vietnam.

Prof. Dinh: I have mentioned this before, but I would like to repeat it: I do not believe that the majority of Americans understand Vietnam at all.

Of course, I want to understand the United States also. We Vietnamese can get confused about the United States. When I came here, I thought I knew a great deal about your country, but what I knew was not completely true. So, you see, many Vietnamese including myself believed in the policies of this country, but we were wrong. We had not read about the Indian wars. We had not read about the conquest of the Philippines. We had not read all the things about the Blacks. As I see it now, we Vietnamese can and must settle our problems by ourselves, without United States interference or assistance.

Gen. Thi: The Pentagon Papers do not mention the Vietnamese directly, or why we have so many problems with the North Vietnamese.

In 1963 and 1964 we had very few enemies in this area. But when the United States decided to send its forces over there, the North Vietnamese sent more forces to balance those forces; then the people heard the President of Vietnam talking about winning the war with the Americans, and this talk continued. Three years ago we had 500 thousand troops, and now we have a million, and they said with that we could win. Well, it turned out we could not win the war then, so how can we win the war now?

The United States government and the South Vietnamese government are making the people very angry. We fight the war, and when you cannot win the war, you continue fighting.

The policy of the United States has not brought democracy to the South Vietnam people. And when the people look at

the government putting so many students and people in jail, who can believe the Americans would allow us to have a democracy?

We have so many problems in South Vietnam, but yet the Americans have asked the South Vietnamese to send forces into Laos.

Now we are looking at the problem officially created by the American CIA, and right now we have approximately 250 thousand North Vietnamese soldiers in South Vietnam. We still have 300 thousand GIs, and we have one million soldiers.

You have all that heavy equipment, and the leadership is repressive. If the Americans leave South Vietnam, I think it will collapse very quickly.

REP. KOCH: I would like to pose this question to Mr. Russo.

You have touched upon the fact that the American public—like all of us here—is very much concerned about the American prisoners of war in North Vietnamese jails. You also went on to describe the South Vietnamese jails and made the same charges against them that we make against the North Vietnamese prisoner-of-war camps. And yet the administration has told us on a number of occasions, and the Red Cross has confirmed it, that the Red Cross is in fact permitted to inspect South Vietnamese prisoner-of-war camps and prisoners. The Red Cross reports that the South Vietnamese are in fact observing the Geneva Convention. Are we being lied to?

MR. RUSSO: I want to be very precise in my response to your question.

First of all, let me say I was in South Vietnam between February of 1965 and September of 1966, and I returned there in September, 1967, remaining until January, 1968, so my direct experience is confined to those periods.

During those periods, I visited prisons, jails and detainment centers in something like twenty-three provinces in Vietnam. To give you some idea of the proportion, there are a total of forty-four provinces in Vietnam.

At that time the South Vietnamese did have a prison in Bien Hoa, very close to Saigon, that was a showcase. According to my understanding, it was built and run especially for the International Red Cross. It was a place for them to visit so they could say they had seen the situation, that they had been inside of Vietnam prisons.

But in prisons throughout the country, the conditions were, I would say, horrible. We interviewed prisoners for our study. The jail cells were hardly big enough to contain a man, they smelled terrible, and I tasted some of the food they were given to eat—it was barely edible.

The same conditions existed throughout much of South Vietnam. And prisoners who made it to the jails, according to the stories that I heard, were lucky. Quite often they were summarily executed on the battlefield or in transit between the battlefield and the prison.

I heard stories about times when the jails became overcrowded. When this happened, officials would release the prisoners, because they knew, as everybody knew, that quite often these people were merely innocent peasants who had simply been rounded up at random.

On one occasion, I met a peasant who told me he had been put in jail with no charge, no charge at all, in 1958. When I talked to him, it was 1965.

It is my understanding that when prisoners were considered dangerous they were secretly taken out and shot. It is also my understanding that prisoners were routinely tortured.

We have read in detail, in books and journalistic reports throughout the years, how they were tortured, and I have yet

[108]

to see any exaggeration along these lines.

Usually when we went to interview a prisoner, he would at first be very scared, and the jail keeper would warn us that he was dangerous. There were times when the prisoner was brought to us handcuffed and blindfolded; we refused to interview prisoners under these conditions. We insisted, as fully as we could, that a prisoner be untied, that his handcuffs and his blindfold be removed. It would take a long time to develop any rapport with prisoners in situations of this kind, but we did develop a rapport. And after two or three hours, when they saw we meant them no harm and simply wanted to gather information for studies, then the prisoners would begin to trust us. They would tell us quite openly the ways in which they had been treated, and it was horrible.

Quite often they asked us to intercede for them to save their lives, but, unfortunately, we had no power. Occasionally I would say to the jail keeper, "He seems a nice person to me, and I hope that you can be more lenient with him." But that is as far as we could go.

I reported this to my supervisors in the Rand Corporation. I reported it to people I talked to in the United States Army. I discussed it with Vietnamese officials. I discussed it with United States officials at the highest level. No one seemed to care.

REP. KOCH: Am I correct then in thinking that the policy always has been that the United States Army turns over prisoners of war to the South Vietnamese—that it does not have prisoners of war?

MR. RUSSO: As I said, I have not been to South Vietnam since 1968, but my understanding is that the United States does turn over its prisoners to the South Vietnamese after it

has exploited them as much as possible for intelligence purposes.

In the Saigon area is a jail that is an adjunct to what is called, I believe, the National Interrogation Center. According to my understanding, it is funded and supported by the CIA, and there were a lot of Americans there who seemed to me at the time to be running the show. So I would say that in that situation prisoners were kept by Americans. I do not know if that is still the case. One American there told me in great detail how he used methods of physical torture to extract information from Vietnamese prisoners. He related, for example, how a prisoner was hung by his feet from a tree limb, and how piano wire was looped about his genitals and slowly tightened. That prisoner, he told me, never did talk. This same American told how he got another prisoner to talk by threatening to kill his mother.

Ms. Fredrick: I would like to add a footnote. I think it is very interesting to realize there is little difficulty in finding POWs in Vietnam. In addition to finding people who are prisoners of war in theory, anywhere from 100 thousand to 200 thousand are political prisoners, who, because they have been in favor of peace, have been charged and placed in prison; and they are in fact prisoners of war. I refer not just to men, but to women with infants, and very old people.

This is something our administration has been aware of. You should know that the Congress has provided money for this kind of thing. Something like 120 thousand dollars will be provided this year for so-called security measures, which means we are spending six times more for policing those in favor of peace than we are spending for education in South Vietnam.

Also, there are construction firms building new Tiger Cages,

similar to those discovered by Don Luce and Congressmen
Anderson and Hawkins at Con Son. This we should be aware
of too.

REP. DOW: Along that line, it has been said that the Saigon
regime has 100 thousand political prisoners in jails in South
Vietnam. Do you think that is about right?

MS. FREDRICK: I would imagine it is considerably more than
that.

REP. DOW: If they have that number of prisoners, and if
they are of the opposition parties, it might color the election.
It would be equivalent to our having a million Republicans (or
Democrats, as the case may be) in jail in this country, would
it not? In that case, a fair election could not be conducted
because most of the leaders of the political party in opposition
would probably be in jail.

MR. LONG: In the big prisons near Saigon you have approximately 35 thousand political prisoners. In the island of Phu
Quoc you have about 50 thousand or 60 thousand and then
in the prison island of Con Son there are about 40 thousand.
That does not include the big detention camps, and there are
many other jails throughout the country. The conditions of the
so-called political prisoners are often bad, because they are
often put in Tiger Cages, moreover, the Saigon regime uses
regular criminals to watch over these people. What is even
worse is that United States Military Police are involved in
this, and United States advisors are present. In fact, AID advisors are present in most of the big prisons of Vietnam. I
would like to make this fact known.

REP. DOW: In the past five months I have had occasion to
participate in a good many sessions in which former Vietnam

[111]

veterans recounted their experiences. Many of these men have said, in describing South Vietnamese tortures which they witnessed, that they have seen them beat prisoners, push them out of helicopters and apply electric shocks to their genitals. Senator Hatfield has entered the testimony of some soldiers into the *Congressional Record.* Congressman Zablocki's committee also has some testimony on this. So anybody interested in the question might want to look through that.

REP. KOCH: Ms. Fredrick, I am in accord with you that they are all prisoners, whether they are prisoners of war in a technical sense or in a political sense, and that they all ought to be accorded at least humane treatment as provided for in the Geneva Convention. To permit our administration to ease out on the technicality that the Geneva Convention only covers prisoners of war is something I cannot go along with.

I want to get a response from Mr. Russo that the people he was talking about are those prisoners of war (even in the strict definition of this term) who should be covered by the Geneva Convention and yet are not accorded this protection by the South Vietnamese, or in effect by the United States, because we have transported them and given them to the South Vietnamese. Is that a fair statement?

MR. RUSSO: I would answer that by defining the types of prisoners I came in contact with. For the most part, these were people who had fought with the Viet Cong or with the North Vietnamese armies; they were brutalized routinely, and this was done with full knowledge of the Americans.

In addition, there were people who had been thrown into jail for any number of reasons. Sometimes we would see people who were informers. They were sent to us to be interviewed, and they would say, "I am not really a Viet Cong. I

am here because the Chief paid me to come into the prison to inform you of what is going on."

There were also political prisoners (opposed to the government but neither Viet Cong nor North Vietnamese), and, as I said, there was the gentleman I talked to who had been in there seven years with no charge. I had no way of telling what kind of prisoner he was.

The people in the jails of South Vietnam are the people of Vietnam.

MR. HOSTETTER: It becomes very evident from even a cursory reading of the Pentagon Papers that the people of the United States have been basically deceived about where the Vietnamese people stand. We have been deceived in being told that the Vietnamese people supported the Diem government. We have been deceived in being told that the Vietnamese people have supported every government since then in South Vietnam. It has been very clear that this was not the case. Every government in South Vietnam since 1945 has been unpopular with the Vietnamese people.

How does it happen that governments which are very unpopular with the people of South Vietnam have been successfully presented to the American people as governments representative of the Vietnamese people?

The only way in which this can be done is through political repression—the suppression of the right of individuals to speak out for what they truly feel, and tell what they truly believe. This repression has been going on for many years.

I have spent three years in South Vietnam, working with Vietnam Christian Service in refugee camps, prisons, and with students, watching how political repression works. The only way in which it will be possible for the United States to get out of South Vietnam, short of military defeat or total eco-

nomic chaos in this country, will be for us to allow the South Vietnamese people to speak out and express how they really feel about the Americans, their government and the war.

This means that we will have to put an end to our aid of repression in South Vietnam. One of the foremost examples of repression, which is currently very visible, is the case of the South Vietnamese student leader Huynh Tan Mam.

Huynh Tan Mam was a democratically elected president of the South Vietnamese Student Union. He was elected by a majority vote of the student unions of all of the universities in South Vietnam. Last August, Mam was arrested during the fourth annual National Student Congress, at which the students were discussing the role of the military in the university. He, along with 117 other students, was arrested, tortured and thrown into prison.

The case was brought before a South Vietnamese civilian court. The court immediately threw out the case for lack of evidence. Since the case could not be prosecuted under the civilian law, it was then taken to the Mobile Military Field Courts—the special courts which were set up by the Diem government to take care of all political opposition.

Mam was convicted of treason by the Military Field Court, but before any sentence was enacted, the Saigon Supreme Court, in a very daring and courageous move, decided that the Military Field Courts were unconstitutional.

It overturned the decision and said that Mam and the rest of the students were free. But the students were not released. The United States government, which speaks so nobly about the democracy we are fighting for in Vietnam, took no action to insure that they were released.

There were protests from a number of the PTA groups, faculty, religious groups, artists and intellectuals in South Vietnam. Still nothing was done. Finally, on September 17,

Mam and twelve other students vowed they would fast to death until they were released.

It was only through the intense pressure which was brought to bear by students, parents and many of the citizens of Saigon that Mam and the other students were finally released. Since then, Mam has been active in almost every antiwar demonstration and movement.

At the time of the invasion of Cambodia, Mam and many others spoke out against the widening of the war and the killing of Vietnamese by a government that was supported by the United States and South Vietnamese governments. At the time of the rebombing of North Vietnam, Mam and many others spoke out against the expansion of the war. At the time of the invasion of Laos, he spoke out, demanding that the United States no longer use the Vietnamese as their bait for spreading their war into other countries.

Then, last winter, Mam took the ultimate, courageous step. He actually signed the Peoples Peace Treaty, a document drawn up and signed by students from the United States, South Vietnam and North Vietnam. The document was originally drafted in South Vietnam and then taken to Hanoi, where it was revised with the aid of Hanoi's student delegation. Eventually a document was arrived at which was agreeable to the students of North and South Vietnam. Mam had the courage to stand up and say the Vietnamese should be allowed to speak up for what they believed and to run their own country.

In consequence, Mam has again been indicted for treason, and if all went as planned, he was supposed to have been tried July 27, once again by the Military Field Court in Saigon. [10]

[10] The trial Cynthia Fredrick and Doug Hostetter both talk about as scheduled never took place on July 27, 1971. Some time after that date Mam was released, only to be re-arrested in October immediately after the Vietnamese elections. He was

Many Americans say, "Yes, but this is an internal problem. The South Vietnamese government has a right to do what it pleases." Many Americans feel that if a man has committed treason, the South Vietnamese government has a right to try him.

The Pentagon Papers have once again revealed the fallacy of this rationale. America has been involved from the beginning to the end setting up, supplying and supporting the Saigon government. We are, in fact, totally responsible for everything done by that government.

In 1963, we set up a force of sixteen thousand men in Saigon which had been trained and fully equipped by the Michigan State University Police Project. By 1970, this had grown to 97 thousand, and according to United States AID statistics, the police force for next year will be 122 thousand.

The entire budget for the Saigon police force is supplied by American money. We are responsible for every suppression of the freedom of speech in South Vietnam, despite the fact that President Nixon and the South Vietnamese government have always claimed to be fighting for the right of self-determination of the Vietnamese people.

These are merely empty words so long as we allow political trials to take place in South Vietnam, so long as we allow the Phoenix program to continue to assassinate elected civilian

---

then released later in October. Once again in early January of 1972 Mam was re-arrested, and is still in prison. His physical condition is very poor; he reportedly loses consciousness from time to time; and students who observed him in prison say he has been tortured. According to the State Department, the Saigon government is "out to get him" this time. Since the Saigon government has indicated that it wants to see Mam executed, it is expected that he will be tried and executed on charges of treason and rebellion.

officials in areas not controlled by the Saigon government—
through programs set up and paid for by United States money.

Until we are ready to change the inconsistencies, to demand a total stop to all political trials and all political assassi-
nations, until then, all of our talk about the Vietnamese ability
to choose for themselves and have self-determination is essentially meaningless and self-deceptive.

BISHOP MOORE: Mr. Ellsberg spoke of some of the strange
ironies of history for the younger generation. Our generation
has even stranger ones. About thirty years ago I was in the
Pacific as an infantry officer in the Marine Corps in Guadalca-
nal, fighting against facism, and I was wounded and came
home.

I did not have a chance to go back across the Pacific until
last year when I visited Saigon with a student and religious
delegation on a peace mission. We were there to investigate
the activity of the peace groups in Saigon and also the extent
of the repression against them there.

I would just like to make, very briefly, two or three points.
First of all, the obvious point that has already been made today, but must be made again, and again, and again, is that we
do not support freedom in South Vietnam, nor do we support
self-determination.

The Thieu regime is repressive. We were there a week and
were followed by the secret police all day and all night.
Groups we wanted to meet with were often afraid and had to
meet with us secretly.

We actually saw wounds: people with fingernails ripped
apart by the insertion of bamboo splinters in the torture center run by the police. I hate to introduce this kind of terrible
accounting but I think I must.

[117]

I will just read a short paragraph, a quotation from one of the students we interviewed when we were over there.

"They beat me from both sides," he said, "and when I bent down, they kneed me. Those times, blood often came out of my mouth, but still I would not sign their papers." The papers he was asked to sign stated that he was a Communist. He was a peace worker.

> Then they put bamboo splinters under my fingernails, and they attached electrodes to my ears, my tongue and my private parts. Then they fed me water in my mouth, tramping on my stomach when I became bloated with the water. Then they hung me from the ceiling and extinguished lighted cigarettes on my nipples and on my private parts. Finally, they injected medicine into me, took my hand and signed a paper. Later they showed me the paper. They said I had a liaison with the Communists.

We saw the results of these tortures. We saw Mr. Mam whose history Mr. Hostetter has just described to you. His health is all but shattered and he is deaf in one ear as a result of the tortures he underwent.

We had one unforgettable experience which I shall tell you about. We were asked to stand with the students and clergy of the Buddhist and Catholic faiths, mothers and other peace-movement people in what we would call a demonstration and they call a manifestation.

It was peaceful. The purpose of it was merely to present a letter of protest to our embassy and for the Vietnamese to proceed to and stand before the Presidential Palace. They felt that perhaps if we stood beside them, the demonstration would be allowed.

When we came down the street toward our embassy we saw that the street was barricaded by the South Vietnamese police. When we were within about two hundred yards of them,

[118]

they opened fire on us with gas bombs. We tried to pull back to get away from the gas and found they had cut off our rear and were firing on us from the rear as well. We were trapped in a small city block. Finally we broke our way through and gained escape. There were women and children with us.

It was a very disagreeable situation—the punitive use of tear gas—but minor in comparison with the terrible tortures to which the political prisoners have been subjected.

And these are just several of thousands of instances of repression in a regime which we are theoretically supporting for freedom's sake.

My second main point is that Vietnamization perpetuates this regime whether we remain in Vietnam or not. By supplying it with arms and other equipment, we are perpetuating this regime against the Vietnamese people's deep longing for unification and self-determination.

In this sense, we are working against anti-Communism. In the words of the Buddhist monk, Dik Van Minh, "Unless people respect their government, they have no spirit to fight against Communists." Because we support a government for which they cannot have respect, we cannot expect the South Vietnamese people to have the spirit to fight against Communism. Therefore, our present policy operates against our alleged goals. In other words, it operates against freedom. And so I would like to raise before all of you two or three very obvious issues we still have to wrestle with.

What does really motivate our continued support of the Thieu regime? And if we do, indeed, pull out our troops, what motivates our continued support of that regime with arms and other equipment?

Which brings us to another question: What motivates our whole foreign policy as evidenced quite clearly by the places like Greece and Spain where Vice President Agnew stopped on

his recent trip? Whose interests does our foreign policy represent? Does it represent your interests and mine? Certainly not mine. If it does not represent our interests, what segment of the American population does our foreign policy represent? Vietnam is just one tragic result of our foreign policy, a policy which is global and could produce other Vietnams in other parts of the world.

If indeed we are fortunate enough to withdraw from Southeast Asia and to cut down our armament appropriations, it is not too soon to begin an urgent campaign toward the reordering of the priorities of this country. Otherwise, when the war is over, we will simply not spend as much money or we will continue to spend our money, not for our cities, not for education, not for poverty, but for some other foreign political adventure or military-equipment adventure at home.

MR. LUCE: What has been made most clear to me in rereading the Pentagon Papers is that we have never really been concerned about the real needs and desires of the Vietnamese people.

If you go through the names of the important decision makers as they appear in the Pentagon Papers, you will find that we have never had anyone at the decision making level who could speak Vietnamese.

To my knowledge we have never had an ambassador in Vietnam who could say hello in Vietnamese. I remember, some time ago, the Secretary of Defense, Mr. McNamara, visited Vietnam. He intended to say, "Long live Vietnam," but what he actually said was, "The Southern duck wants to lie down."

I would say the lessons to be learned for both the present and the future, with respect to not only Vietnam but to all of the countries we are working in and that we are trying to

understand, is that we ought to have some people at the decision-making level, actually all of the people at the decision-making level in those countries, capable of speaking the languages of those countries.

We haven't taken into consideration the great masses of people. As you read the Pentagon Papers, you realize that our decision makers were preoccupied with matters which were completely different from what the Vietnamese people themselves were talking about.

During the 1960's the Vietnamese were talking about defoliation; they were talking about the bombing in South Vietnam; they were talking about the refugee situation and being removed from their villages. The Pentagon Papers talk about relationships between the generals.

I know that villages the International Voluntary Services (IVS) members worked in were bombed. I remember talking with villagers, and they told me about the planes, and they said, "We used to lie down when we saw a plane. Now we stand up and always keep our heads pointed in the direction of the airplanes because we make a smaller target."

I think this is the kind of thing government officials have to know to really understand how Vietnamese feel on a day-by-day basis. Officials are talking about elections, and I would remind you that right now the United States government is spending thirty million dollars on a police force that is responsible for the imprisonment of 100 thousand political prisoners in South Vietnam. These include the runner-up in the last elections. They include the Congressman who received the highest majority of votes of any Congressman in South Vietnam. I know of three newspaper editors who are in the jails of South Vietnam.

I think also, if you wish to talk about the future, we ought to stop building prisons for political prisoners. After Congress-

man Anderson and Congressman Hawkins and I went to Con Son Island, the Tiger Cages were done away with. Now, they have been rebuilt with a 400 thousand dollar United States contract by Raymond, Morrison, Knutson-Brown, Root and Jones.

Finally, I would just say this. I have been traveling around the United States since I came back in May, and I find you can't be as cynical about conditions abroad as our government officials have been without also becoming cynical about conditions here in the United States. I am finding that the vast majority of the Americans I talk with feel that their government isn't listening to them, that there is absolutely nothing they can do. A tremendous amount of discouragement exists right here in the United States because of the same kind of disregard for American people, as for the Vietnamese over there.

I wonder how the Pentagon Papers would read if they were reporting on the attitudes in the higher levels of our government about what the poor people are saying and what the people in the minority groups in the United States are saying.

PROF. MARR: I wanted to address myself to one aspect which has come up in the news in the last three or four weeks regarding United States activities and possible activities in Vietnam. This is the elections themselves.

I'd like to concentrate especially on General Minh's proposal to Americans that the United States government involve itself in the upcoming elections in some sort of a supervisory role.

As the news media reported in early July, General Duong Van Minh is asking for United States pressure on the Thieu regime to "assure fair elections" for the South Vietnamese elections this coming October.

[122]

At first sight, many Americans will see this as a legitimate request, given our democratic ideals, given our actual long-time involvement in the political affairs of Vietnam, and especially given General Minh's accurate portrayal of just how badly the 1967 elections were rigged with the knowledge and consent of the United States.

Indeed, even some Americans who favor setting a date for our total withdrawal from Indochina will react favorably to General Minh's idea, perhaps because they think that, as president, General Minh could help us extricate ourselves more gracefully from that area.

A few will hope, too, that by somehow "guaranteeing" these elections we can wipe the sordid past clean and perform a single, last, beneficial act for the Vietnamese people. What I would like to say here is that it just won't work.

It makes sense in the American political environment, but it bears little or no relationship to political realities in South Vietnam. Most important, we have to ask why General Minh has to make these pleas to an American constituency.

After all, it is Vietnamese, not Americans, who are going to be doing the voting or not voting in October. For a variety of reasons, not all of them of their own making, the so-called "Third Force" in South Vietnam has failed over the years to develop a viable, independent political base between the NLF on the left and the established Saigon regime on the right.

Thus, as it stands today, the NLF remains the only major political organization that can compete and succeed in South Vietnam without some form and degree of United States support. This has induced the Vietnamese, as General Minh himself admits, to choose repeatedly between association with the NLF on the one hand, and dependence on the United States on the other.

This is why General Minh is following the path of his pre-

decessors, Ngo Dinh Diem, Nguyen Khanh, Nguyen Cao Ky, and Nguyen Van Thieu, by asking for help from the United States. He wants the United States to remove its support from those sitting in power in Saigon.

And he wants this done prior to the elections, thus putting the province- and district chiefs, the regimental- and battalion commanders, the local security personnel and all the rest into such a quandary that many or most of them will transfer their personal allegiance to him.

They will then proceed to get out the vote for Big Minh in the same fashion that was planned for President Thieu, using techniques that will make Boss Tweed and Tammany Hall look like rank amateurs.

If General Minh wins, he has already said that he will oppose a coalition government with the NLF, hardly surprising, given the essential similarity of his political base to that of President Thieu.

In short, the October elections in South Vietnam are not likely to solve anything, with or without United States support to one candidate or another. There is no reason to think that one last adventurous fling in Vietnamese domestic politics will produce anyone better than our previous friends Diem, Khanh, Ky and Thieu.

On the other hand, if we immediately set a firm date for total withdrawal of United States forces, then no Vietnamese presidential candidate can claim that we are either supporting him or rejecting him. Each will be on his own, for the very first time. And the United States will have assimilated its most important lesson from Vietnam: constant dabbling in the internal political affairs of another country usually ends up making things worse rather than better.

Mr. Truong: I would like to address myself to what should

be the course of the United States control of Vietnamization.

I think one of the basic points is that the United States seems to have hit a snag on the issue of giving a reasonable chance to the Saigon regime to survive and stand on its own feet. That issue is closely related to the issue of a coalition government for South Vietnam.

I think when one talks about giving the South Vietnamese regime a reasonable chance to stand on its own feet, one should put it in the context of whether the United States has been able to give to the South Vietnamese the right to self-determination, for the given objective has never been accomplished during all these years of American military and political presence in South Vietnam.

My view, and I think I can add to that my father's views and the views of those who have worked for him, is that the United States did not achieve anything in South Vietnam. How can this country claim to protect the rights to self-determination of 17.8 million South Vietnamese when it can not guarantee the rights to freedom of speech of those 100 thousand political prisoners who are now rotting in jail for having spoken out for a political settlement in Vietnam?

I have some material here about the last election—in 1967. For instance, in my father's native province, the province of Binh Dinh which is considered a heavy Viet Cong stronghold, we had an observer, who happened to be my uncle, at the provincial police station. We were leading by some 40 thousand votes when the voting stations were closed and the voting ballots had been counted.

My uncle went away for about an hour and fifteen minutes. When he returned, the Thieu ticket was suddenly leading by some 56 thousand votes. Somehow, at Binh Dinh the Thieu-Ky ticket managed to win by a margin of some 60 thou-

sand votes, and two days later the province chief was removed.

The province chief has provided us with written testimony about why he was removed. That was only one of the incidents. We have some 1,060 *procès-verbals* on the subject of falsified signatures, wherein it seems that there was an average of 500 suspicious ballots at each of the 8,824 police stations in the fifty provinces and municipalities.

All this evidence was filed with the validation committee of the Assembly in 1967 after the elections. But somehow, despite the evidence, the Thieu-Ky regime forced the validation committee and the Assembly to vote for the validation of the Thieu-Ky ticket.

Also, General Loan, who was then the head of the police forces, came to talk to my father and offered him quite a sizeable sum, somewhere between one million and two-and-a-half million dollars, asking him to accept the money and withdraw in favor of the Thieu-Ky ticket.

There were also similar attempts to buy off other presidential candidates. So, in the light of this, it is interesting to focus upon the forthcoming presidential elections and how the campaign is being run.

One of the aides of President Thieu declared recently that the government would be ready to help General Minh just to make the elections cheerful. So, to that extent, when we talk about a reasonable chance to give the Saigon government the ability to stand on its own feet, the question that one should ask, and I think the people around President Nixon should also ask, is whether the whole American-conceived and American-enforced electoral process is applicable to South Vietnam and whether the people of South Vietnam really want that.

One can conclude—on the basis of all the electoral games the United States has been playing with the few privileged peo-

ple who are in power in South Vietnam—that the Vietnamese people don't really care one way or the other about the present electoral process, and look on it as a confirmation of the rottenness, corruption and unrepresentativeness of the Thieu regime.

It tends to lead one to the argument that a massive social revolution and political upheaval will be needed in order to bring really good Vietnamese leadership to the top. To reelect Thieu will be useless, or even some person like General Minh, who might replace Thieu to make the situation more appealing for American consumption. I think the only way that one can see how the course of the United States withdrawal should be from South Vietnam is really to explore what a coalition government in South Vietnam would involve.

I would like to cite Henry Kissinger's statement in his article for Foreign Affairs of January 1969, in which he looked at the coalition issue in two ways: one, as a means of legitimizing partition as a disguise for continuing the civil war, that case being the Laotian example; the other as a true coalition government attempting to govern the whole country. He further said the issue here is whether the United States should be party to an attempt to impose a coalition government on South Vietnam.

I think the issue here to most Vietnamese is whether this country should continue to impose either General Thieu or perhaps, to make the regime more appealing, to impose Minh or anybody else on the people of South Vietnam.

I think that there is some common ground here between what Henry Kissinger said and a point made by the PRG in Paris recently—one finds some amount of consensus here. That is, while the United States should not try to impose a coalition government on South Vietnam, it is also true that the

United States should stop imposing the Thieu regime on the people of South Vietnam.

I think this country could certainly give South Vietnam a reasonable chance to stand on its own by setting a deadline for the withdrawal of all United States troops before the October 3 elections in which General Thieu and General Minh are participants. That will show very clearly which way the local political forces would move.

Whether the United States likes it or not, I think the only way to end the war, after setting a date for withdrawing, is to allow the South Vietnamese to work out a certain degree of political accommodation through the solution of a coalition government.

MR. LONG: From the Pentagon Papers we have learned that because of total disregard for Vietnamese history, the United States has inflicted unprecedented suffering on a people whose only crime is their desire to be independent and to bring social justice to their country.

We have learned that this complete lack of regard for human suffering on the part of the policy makers of the United States has resulted in a war in which the most atrocious of modern methods has been employed against the innocent people of Indochina, thereby making anything short of total withdrawal of all United States and other foreign troops totally unacceptable to these people.

The question, therefore, is how can the American public and Congress put pressure on the Nixon administration to end this senseless war? One way is to address ourselves to the central issues, to inform the American public that the administration does not want to end the war.

I think it is very relevant to talk about the seven-point peace plan proposed by the other side. It seems to me that not

only has the President of this country not discussed the seven-point proposal clearly but that the Nixon administration has intentionally denounced that peace proposal.

One of the things that the Congress and informed individuals can do at the present time is point out that the seven-point peace proposal meets, in effect, every demand made by the Nixon administration, as well as those made by previous administrations, and that failure on the part of the Nixon administration to agree to any meaningful discussion of that proposal reflects nothing but its desire to seek a military victory or the total destruction of the Indochinese people.

The Nixon administration has said it is very concerned about the security of American troops and also about the fate of the American POWs. The first point precisely guarantees the security of American troops and promises to release all American prisoners if the United States will withdraw from Vietnam. Therefore, the United States does not have to invade Laos or Cambodia, and the United States doesn't have to bomb North Vietnam to protect the American troops.

The other concern of the United States has to do with the problem of world Communism and the Communist domination of Asia. Point four of the seven-point peace proposal states that in the future neither the northern nor southern parts of Vietnam will form military alliances with any foreign country. Nor will any foreign country be allowed to offer protection or establish bases, troops or military personnel in the north or south.

This means that the other side agrees to the neutralization of both North and South Vietnam. It is giving the United States a graceful way out of the war. The United States government can now say to the American people that the other side has capitulated, that they have agreed to become a buffer zone against Communist expansion in Southeast Asia.

It seems to me that when a superpower gets into a war with a small nation and comes out of the war without getting anything at all, that is a disaster. So if the United States gets out of Vietnam right now without showing the American people they have gained anything at all, the war will be viewed as a big failure. As I recall, the United States Assistant Defense Secretary in 1964–1965 stated that the chief objective of the American effort in Vietnam was to come out of that conflict without embarrassment.[11] It is precisely for this reason that the seven-point peace proposal is important.

And finally, point two of the seven-point peace proposal guarantees that in the future there will be no political reprisals. This answers the question about the possibility of a blood bath.

REP. RYAN: Although the seven-point proposal may answer many of the conditions, so to speak, it does not deal with the one point which the President has used to explain continued American support and his Vietnamization policy, and that is, a reasonable chance for South Vietnam to survive.

MR. LONG: Yes. After the defeat of the French in 1954, the Saigon army was a defeated army of only 50 thousand men. The United States has built up the army over the years so that it has about a million men now. The United States has pacified the countryside of Vietnam through the use of every possible means at her disposal to try to give the South Vietnam government that reasonable chance.

The United States has had more than ten years to do that, and what has it done? The United States has killed hundreds of thousands of innocent people and made the survivors its enemies.

11 Ibid., pp. 491–492.

In fact, the action of the United States in Vietnam has caused even the Catholic Church in Vietnam to oppose the war. I would suggest to the American people, no matter where you stand, if you are really for peace in Vietnam, stop putting your fingers in the Vietnamese affairs and try to set a date for the withdrawal of all American troops from Vietnam, because history has shown that today's enemies may become tomorrow's friends.

Another thing the American people and Congress can do is to point out that the next election in Vietnam is an attempt by the United States to continue the war in Vietnam even if General Minh were elected. It is well known that General Minh collaborated with the French and that he was most willing to cooperate with the United States in the early sixties.

It is well known that on December 25, 1970, Big Minh declared publicly in Saigon, "Whatever I do will be constitutional. I won't do anything that is unconstitutional." Since the constitution of South Vietnam was drafted with the help of Americans, and since it officially outlaws the National Liberation Front, by having Big Minh elected on the peace ticket and then having him ask for continued United States support, the United States government can score a propaganda coup against the American peace movement and clear the way for continued intervention in Vietnamese affairs.

PROF. MARR: As I read the Vietnamese text of the seven points, which I would assume the NLF considers to be the definitive one, they say that the "procedures" for release will be discussed, not the modalities, if there is a distinction to be made here.

But more important, they say that the release of prisoners and the withdrawals will begin simultaneously, so that what the United States seems to fear would happen would be impos-

sible. That is, troops would be withdrawing and the POWs would be released simultaneously, so I don't see a problem there.

Additionally, if has been said that the NLF and the North Vietnamese have declared the death penalty for brothers and sisters and relatives who were or are on the other side. It is well known that a number of the leaders of the NLF have relatives, even brothers, within the government of South Vietnam and within the army of South Vietnam.

I will just mention one example. One of the high-ranking leaders, the Minister of Health of the Democratic Republic of Vietnam, who died last year, had very close relatives in the government and in the army of South Vietnam, and he remained Minister of Health for many years until his death, not by execution, but from natural causes.

MR. LUCE: I should like to make a comment on the basis of some very simple experiences I had, in terms of the question of whether there will be a blood bath should the United States withdraw. In February of this year I attended a wedding in the fourth largest city of the country. One of the wedding guests was an NLF major who came, congratulated the bride and groom and then joined in the wedding feast.

I think, too, religious ties are extremely important. I would point out that week after week people who are sympathetic to the Saigon government and people who are sympathetic to the NLF are meeting together in the churches and in the pagodas. I know a Buddhist monk in Central Vietnam who invited both local NLF troops and local Saigon government troops to his pagoda, and they shared a meal together and left. The most important Buddhist monk for Central Vietnam, Venerable Don Hau, is with the NLF.

Because of the religious forces and because of the family

[132]

ties, I think the Vietnamese simply want to live together in peace. As long as we are there with our airplanes, soldiers and the rest, the war will go on.

I believe when we leave the people will find peace.

CHAPTER FOUR

U.S. Foreign Policy Appraisal: Implications for the Future

MR. BRANFMAN: I should like, in my opening remarks, to ignore the contingency plans and opinions of Pentagon researchers and concentrate instead on what the Pentagon Papers reveal the United States government has actually done in Laos.

In a July 1961 memo, Colonel Lansdale reports to Ambassador Taylor that "About 9,000 Meo tribesmen have been equipped for guerilla operations. . . . Command control of Meo operations is exercised by the Chief CIA Vientiane with the advice of Chief MAAG Laos." [1]

In the same memo he writes that some ninety-nine Thai special forces have been introduced to work with the Meo, the South Vietnamese have made shallow penetrations into Laos, American military advisors are working widely with the Lao army and the Civil Air Transport is flying arms and men around.

Moreover, the Filipino-run Eastern Construction Company

[1] *The Pentagon Papers*, as published by *The New York Times*. New York: Bantam, 1971, pp. 134–135.

is providing logistics for the Lao army, Operation Brotherhood is providing hospital care throughout Laos, and both have a "measure of control."

He also reports that "there is . . . a local veteran's organization and a grass-roots political operation in Laos, both of which are subject to CIA direction and control and are capable of carrying out propaganda, sabotage and harassment operations." [2]

A large number of memos and cables for the year 1964 reveal the following:

1. In May 1964, the United States began propeller-driven bombing in Laos, in T-28s, piloted by American (working for Air America), Thai and, later, Lao pilots; photo reconnaissance for target selection was begun the same month by American jets from Yankee Team.

2. On December 14, 1964, American Air Force and Navy jets began bombing in Laos.

3. Earlier in the year, teams of South Vietnamese had been parachuted into Laos and captured.

4. On the political front, the United States was opposed to negotiations in Laos on the grounds that this would show weakness and hamper possible cross-border operations.

From 1965 on, Laos is more or less ignored in the Pentagon Papers, apparently because it fell under the aegis of the CIA and State Department, and the backup for American activities in Laos was in Thailand, not South Vietnam.

The one major exception is Secretary of Defense McNamara's paper of May 19, 1967, which reports that

[2] Ibid., p. 135.

In Laos, we average 5,000 attack sorties a month against the infiltration routes and base areas, we fire artillery from South Vietnam against targets in Laos, and we will be providing 3-man leadership for each of 20 12-man U.S.-Vietnamese Special Forces teams that operate to a depth of 20 kilometers into Laos. [3]

All these activities have been expanded, and they continue today, with great impact on the people and nation of Laos:

1. By now the United States has introduced some ten thousand foot-soldiers, special forces and pilots into Laos from Thailand, a traditional enemy of Laos, and one which had occupied more of its territory for longer periods of time than any of its neighbors.

2. The Meo and other American-supported hill tribes, numbering some hundreds of thousands, have been decimated.

3. Some twenty thousand South Vietnamese invaded Laos this February.

4. American bombers have carried out one of the most protracted bombings of civilian targets in history in the two-thirds of Laos controlled by the Pathet Lao, partially or totally- destroying thousands of villages, killing and wounding tens of thousands of civilians, and driving hundreds of thousands underground.

Arguments may rage over whether the United States was legally justified in carrying out these actions, in view of North Vietnamese involvement in Laos. What is beyond dispute, however, is that American actions in Laos—at a cost of billions—have brought unprecedented suffering to that tiny land without guaranteeing American interests; for the other side today controls far more territory and people than it did when the United States began its intervention.

But what perhaps should concern us most as Americans is

[3] Ibid., p. 581.

what the Pentagon Papers tell us about the direction in which our country has moved down the road of totalitarianism since the end of World War II. For the widespread death and destruction wreaked in Laos has been initiated by a tiny group of men in the Executive branch, who have neither consulted nor truthfully informed either Congress or the American people.

One would be hard put to find significant differences between American Executive intervention in Laos, and that of the Soviet Politburo in Hungary or Czechoslovakia. In both cases military activities of a modern superstate are carried out by vast state bureaucracies which are not subject to popular or legislative control.

The basic lesson of the Pentagon Papers is, to quote Senator Fulbright, that a "Presidential Dictatorship" is today executing American foreign policy. And the basic lesson of Laos is that the founding fathers of this Republic were correct in seeking to avoid entrusting the conduct of foreign affairs to any one branch of government.

If the bones of over one million Asians and Americans, the maimed bodies of over two million, the charred ruins of tens of thousands of homes, the waste of over 100 billion dollars, the twisted wreckage of thousands of machines of war, and the ravaged countryside of what was once one of the most beautiful areas of the world, does not teach us that the greatest threat to our democratic traditions comes from the autocratic use of power by our own leaders, then nothing will; if all this does not move Congress to reassert some control over the use of American technology and lives, then nothing will.

And the agony of the people of Indochina will be but a prelude to the agony of all those in this land who refuse to submit to Executive tyranny in the years to come.

[138]

PROF. CHOMSKY: I have a number of reservations in doing what I was asked, namely, to discuss the significance of the Pentagon Papers as a historical document. In the first place, what has been published so far is only a fragment. This raises obvious problems of evaluation. More important, the published fragments reveal the operation of a system of executive decision making that continues to function as before, that still functions within the framework of assumptions that have guided United States policy for more than twenty years. It is the implications for the future that must be our primary concern.

Putting aside these reservations and turning to the historical record, there are a number of points I would like to discuss, if time permits.

In the first place, the Pentagon study fills in certain gaps in our knowledge, for example, in connection with developments in Laos in 1964. Furthermore, the documentary record corroborates certain reasonable conclusions that were based on available evidence, for example, with regard to United States policy concerning negotiations, or the nature and timing of the alleged North Vietnamese aggression in South Vietnam, or the sources of strength of the southern resistance as this was perceived by American planners.

But the most important aspect of the documents is the insight they provide into the mentality of these planners. It is not a pretty picture. It is, in the first instance, a picture of deceit—as when the President stated that "we do not have on my desk at the moment any unfilled requests from General Westmoreland" (February 26, 1966), at a time when there was a request to double the troop commitment of more than 200 thousand, and when the President had on his desk a memorandum from the Secretary of Defense stating that deployments of the kind recommended (to almost 400 thousand

by the end of 1966, perhaps more than 600 thousand in 1967) would be expected to mean a thousand United States troops killed in action per month. The President and his advisors did not consider it appropriate that the American people should be aware of what was in store for them.

It is a picture of shocking ignorance—as witness the repeated statements that a major United States war aim is to keep South Vietnam from Chinese hands. A more profound misunderstanding of Vietnamese nationalism would be difficult to imagine.

It is a picture of remarkable foolishness—as when overflights for dropping leaflets in North Vietnam (recommended May 8, 1961) are designed "to maintain morale of North Vietnamese population," as though the people of North Vietnam, enslaved by their Communist masters, were prayerfully awaiting salvation by American bombers.

Or, a still more extreme case, when the United States Ambassador to Saigon bemoans the "national attribute" which "limits the development of a truly national spirit" among the South Vietnamese (November 1964), and then goes on to muse over "the ability of the Viet Cong continuously to rebuild their units and to make good their losses"—"one of the mysteries of this guerilla war," he writes—and their remarkable morale and recuperative powers, for which "we still find no plausible explanation."

He cannot comprehend that the source of Viet Cong resilience may be precisely a national attribute, deeply rooted in the peasant society that we have systematically destroyed, an attribute that arouses the Vietnamese peasants to resist colonial domination.

It is a picture of callous disregard for the victims of American terror, as when the President's Special Assistant for National Security Affairs explains that a program of sustained

bombing will be relatively cheap, particularly in light of the fact that it will demonstrate "U.S. willingness to employ this new norm in counter-insurgency" if it becomes necessary to suppress other such "adventures" (M. Bundy, February 7, 1965).

More important still, the record reveals the inner workings of a conspiracy to engage the United States in an ever-expanding war of aggression, in flagrant violation of the supreme law of the land, which requires the Executive to rely on negotiations and other pacific means and to refrain from the threat or use of force. In contrast, the conspirators were determined to avoid "premature negotiations" until the use of force had compelled the "enemy" to capitulate, and to order his "proxies" to surrender as well. What we find, in short, is exactly what one should expect of a system of centralized power, insulated from public scrutiny or democratic control.

Thomas Jefferson warned that if citizens "become inattentive to the public affairs" the government will "all become wolves." For a generation, there has been a forced inattention to public affairs in the realm of foreign policy. The American public has been so intensely indoctrinated and rendered so inert that the Executive, as might be anticipated, can become a conspiracy of international predators.

Since little has changed in this regard, we can further anticipate that the grim story revealed in the Pentagon study will be relived in the future, and not only in Indochina.

To my mind, one of the most depressing paragraphs in the Pentagon Papers is the one in which the analyst explains President Johnson's change of tactics in March of 1968. He explains that "large and growing elements of the American public" were unwilling to accept the cost of the war and "would strongly protest a large increase in that cost." If the analyst is correct, then the public is at one with the Executive branch in

its almost exclusive concern with the costs to us of continued aggression.

I personally doubt the accuracy of this assessment, but I think that President Nixon is counting on it, and is hoping that a less costly technological war, with sensors and data processing and mercenaries in place of GI's, and bombing and automated fire control instead of Westmoreland's "meatgrinder," may still succeed in destroying the "political infrastructure of the enemy" and guaranteeing to the Vietnamese and their neighbors the particular variety of independence that the United States Executive is willing to tolerate. If he is correct, then this study might just as well gather dust in the vaults of the Pentagon.

HON. SEN. GRUENING: For those of us who were early opponents of this monstrous and utterly inexcusable war in Southeast Asia, the Pentagon Papers have brought no new revelations except in spelling out the details.

While we did not know then that we were being lied to by those in high office, we did discover this through investigations which were conducted before the publication of the Pentagon Papers. But their publication is nevertheless enormously helpful in that it informs the American public, which has heretofore not had the opportunity to discover how they have been betrayed, how they have been lied to. The American people can easily infer from the Pentagon papers that this lying process and this deception continue. And that is the most serious aspect of it all.

We know, for instance, that President Nixon, when he was a candidate for office, promised us that he would stop the war. He declared he had a formula, but he could not reveal it because to do so would interfere with the Paris talks. On the basis of this promise, he was elected by a small margin. But far from ending the war, he has in fact widened it.

He extended the war from South Vietnam into Laos and Cambodia. He extended the monstrous performance of shelling villages from the air and steadily killing hundreds of thousands of innocent people, a crime just as great as the killings of a score of visible men by a second lieutenant. This is one of the important aspects of the Pentagon Papers that, hopefully, it will alert American opinion and, through that alerting, bring some pressure to bear on Congress, which has a very large responsibility for our participation in the war, just as much, in fact, as the Executive branch. For the Congress has throughout voted the appropriations to carry on this war. So I am extremely hopeful that the revelations of the Pentagon Papers will carry further implications that will lead to much needed reform especially in the area of secrecy. Hopefully, there will be greater communication with the Senate, which under the Constitution is given the power to advise the Executive, a power which has been largely ignored in recent years, partly through the seizure of power by the Executive branch and partly through the unwise renunciation by the Senate of that power.

Now, we should know by this time that this war, which has been carried on allegedly as an action to prevent aggression, was really a war of aggression on the part of the United States. We were the aggressors. We went down there, halfway round the world, and barged into a civil war which we had a large part in precipitating, and we used all of the methods that we condemned Hitler, Mussolini and Stalin for using a generation ago. We are doing what they did, with only one difference.

Hitler believed that the master race, the German people, was destined to rule over the lesser of human species. Mussolini was certainly sincere in his belief that fascism was a method superior to liberty, and Stalin undoubtedly felt that Communism was the way of the future, and this, in their

[143]

views, justified their actions. But what we do, we do in the name of liberation. We do it in the name of self-determination, thereby adding hypocrisy to our other sins, and this is something the American people should know, because it is a betrayal of everything they have stood for throughout the past.

We have made many errors, but never before have we been systematically deceived by three successive presidents. And one can be completely nonpartisan in this matter, because it includes both Republicans and Democrats—both are equally guilty. This is the lesson of the Pentagon Papers. I hope it will have the effect of getting the American people to recapture some of the power that has been taken from them and which has been lodged in wholly unworthy hands. I hope those in high office will find oppressive the thought that the blood of fifty thousand American boys and of hundreds of thousands of Vietnamese lies upon their heads. Again that can also be said without partisanship because it includes the presidents of both parties.

So let us hope the Pentagon Papers will really bring about a new liberation of the spirit, and new determination of the American people to take back their government, and make it truly a government by consent of the governed.

REP. ECKHARDT: Mr. Gurtov, you participated in the Pentagon Papers studies, which to my knowledge were initially undertaken to evaluate the history of and reasons for our involvement in the Vietnam war. Toward whom was the study directed?

PROF. GURTOV: I think most of the information on that is public, and that which is public strikes me as accurate, at least as accurate as I know it to be; namely, that Secretary Mc-

Namara was the person who commissioned the study, in the belief, I imagine, that it was important for him at that rather late stage in the game to have more information.

As I said, I was struck at the time and I'm still struck very forcefully by the belatedness of our coming to grips with the history of United States decision making on the war.

To judge from the number of original copies that the press has indicated were actually produced, which runs anywhere between six and fifteen, it would seem that the Secretary was not interested in disseminating the study and was interested in seeing that only the very highest officials in the administration would have an opportunity to read it.

As we know, the study, which originally was supposed to have been completed in only three or four months actually wound up taking as long as a year and a half before it was finally approved, and by that time, the Secretary was no longer part of the administration.

To the best of my knowledge, no more than a few people—prior to its publication in *The New York Times* and other newspapers—actually read the study in its entirety or in substantial part. And so far as I know, Secretary McNamara himself did not see it; he was not among those very few. Nor, it may be, was his successor, Secretary Clifford. I think I would draw from all of this, aside from the ludicrousness of any decision to make a lengthy study of that kind when Vietnam was so pressing a matter, that it is only because *The New York Times* and other newspapers had the courage to publish those papers that a wide number of people in the administration actually had the impetus to read them.

It was *The New York Times* and other newspapers that made the Pentagon documents newsworthy and important. I think this is one of the strongest arguments that can be made in favor of having the documents published.

[145]

REP. DRINAN: I direct this question to anyone who might have an answer.

Unfortunately, there is no index for the entire set of documents, and I am wondering whether what we know now about the CIA in any way differs from what we knew before. It was a surprise to learn that the CIA had apparently predicted at an early time that the so-called domino theory was specious. Unfortunately, that was not revealed to anyone in the world prior to the publication of the Pentagon Papers.

We have documentation here regarding the activities of a Colonel Lansdale in 1964. He was in Hanoi with a team of CIA agents, who, it appears, contaminated the water supply and sabotaged the railroads.

I wonder if anyone who has been working on these papers could tell us, briefly, what fresh information we now have about the CIA and its activities.

PROF. GURTOV: I will say a few words, but not as an expert on the CIA. I do think that the study validly portrays the analysts in the CIA, as distinct from its agents abroad, in a favorable light.

I think it is interesting that despite all we are told about the CIA, that, really, it was one of the few branches of the American bureaucracy that came to grips with some of the fundamental assumptions about administration policy, including the domino theory, the strategy of rooting out the infrastructure of the Viet Cong, and the bombing strategy begun in 1965.

I hope that this will result in a new appreciation of the fact that in Washington, as distinct from abroad, there are a number of very capable people in the Central Intelligence Agency at the working level. Unfortunately, however, it is as usual—and very disturbing—to learn that when the Central Intelligence Agency or some part of it was commissioned to make these

studies, and when it then came back with reports that clearly challenged some of the fundamentals underlining our policy in Vietnam and was against going along with it, it was ignored along with anybody else who happened to hold views contrary to those of the administration.

MR. BRANFMAN: I think it is very important to complement what Mr. Gurtov just said, by pointing out that perhaps the best way to look at the CIA is in terms of these fundamental distinctions between the analyst here and the operative in the field. I think what Mr. Gurtov said no doubt applies accurately to the analyst. But if we look at Laos we see a very different approach to the problem taken by the CIA in the field.

It is my impression that the CIA today exercises functional control over the war in Laos. One, it controls the ground army which does most of the fighting. Two, it has the largest say during the target meetings in what will be bombed and what will not be bombed. Three, it acts as a major liaison between the government and the Americans in day-to-day contacts. And four, the most important way the CIA controls American policy in Laos is through its monopoly over the information that comes from the Pathet Lao forces. When the CIA delivers reports, the rest of the policy makers have to take that report or leave it.

In general, the CIA does not acknowledge its sources. I might also say, in passing, and I cannot document this, but it is based on my conversations with refugees, that we have had reports of water supplies being poisoned by the Meo guerrillas, which would be under the control of the CIA. We have also had reports of some kind of silver paper that is dropped on the ground and causes burns or blisters on contact. It can be deadly to children. And, reportedly, when water strikes this

silver paper, it is absorbed by the grass and poisons the plants.

I would like to say one last thing. I think one of the most important developments—the key to this whole Vietnam war—is the clandestine army in Laos. This army is composed of some thirty or forty thousand men, Meo or hill troops, Nationalist Chinese and other kinds, which are in turn part of the clandestine army in Thailand—which has a similar number—and also in Cambodia and in South Vietnam. Now, this comes to at least a hundred thousand Asians, all directed by the CIA, who are responsible only to the CIA, and not to their sovereign governments. In fact, what we see today is kind of a CIA foreign legion out there in Laos which is doing a good deal of fighting.

REP. DRINAN: None of that is in these documents?

PROF. CHOMSKY: There is material in the documents. If you check in the Bantam book, on page 130, and the following five or ten pages, there is very significant documentation of some of the CIA operations involved in the early stages of what Mr. Branfman was talking about, in that they are taking control of the organization of the Meo tribesmen, and they have dispatched about a hundred Thai operatives for police work in Laos. Their "combat performance" is said to be "outstanding," and CIA control is reported to be "excellent."

You see the use of Filipinos and others, including Americans, at quite an early stage.

In fact, if one looks at the tremendous tragedy which has befallen not only Laos, but other countries, and the Meo in particular, we can trace it back to that kind of decision which made any kind of negotiations impossible, which led directly, step by step, to the kinds of things that Mr. Branfman is discussing.

REP. ABOUREZK: I want to direct this to any of the participants who might be able to answer it.

The Pentagon Papers show a desire on the part of the Johnson administration to go to war in Southeast Asia back in 1964, and also the preparation of the American people for that war, which they probably would not have accepted if it had all been laid out in the open at the time. My question is, do any of you have a recommendation for avoiding this sort of thing in future?

PROF. CHOMSKY: I have a very simple recommendation, and this is one that Senator Gruening has presented very eloquently for many years, that is, we should adhere to our constitution and to our obligations under international law, which require that we avoid entering into this kind of forceful intervention; and that we rely on the United Nations charter, as the law obliges us, refraining from the threat or use of force in international affairs.

The United States has no authority whatsoever, and certainly not the competence, to institute any government or any regime in South Vietnam or any other country, and if we were to accept that principle, as we are legally obligated to do, the question of what went wrong would not arise.

MR. RUSSO: I would like to make one comment. I think we have to recognize that in the past several decades the foreign policy of the United States has been controlled by a small elite. No matter which administration has been in power, there has been a turnover of perhaps only 400 or so people in the major foreign-policy jobs. And I think that this elite group of people who represent the United States in its foreign policy do not represent the American people.

For example, in Saigon I questioned a number of these

people on the subject of morality as they came through. I was interested in what role morality played in their foreign policy. And almost to a man, the answer they gave me was that morality was irrelevant to the conduct of United States foreign affairs.

PROF. GURTOV: Perhaps there is something so fundamentally wrong with the system itself that no mere tactical change can be of value—any more than the various administrations, over many years, thought that tactical changes could resolve their difficulties in Vietnam.

The Pentagon Papers indicate quite clearly that every major figure leading the government of the United States and every major official working in his behalf, regardless of party, shared a certain belief system; shared certain fundamental values about the role of the United States in the world, about the proper place of revolutionary movements; about the threat of Communism and so on.

It was this common value system that molded our policy in a certain way and predetermined policy choices. Which is why, as you read on in the Pentagon Papers, you find so little interest in the option of disengaging, or even any serious interest in the option of de-escalating.

Many people say, in defense of the Pentagon analysts, that is, of the authors of the documents themselves, that these were really only contingency plans. But, of course, that is very important, because, after all, the kinds of contingency plans we see in the documents were authored by people who were all interested in basically the same thing: how to defeat and contain Communism.

Those were the contingency plans that were "live options," as the bureaucrats like to say. Those were the contingency plans that eventually were adopted by presidents because ac-

tion of some kind, toward deeper involvement was the only kind of option that presidents had before them to act upon.

With that remark, however, I would like to make a few general recommendations, for what they are worth. One is that the Congress should consider itself responsible for pressing the administration to reveal the full extent of its policies, and in particular, at the very least, should insist that the administration bring before the relevant bodies of the Congress information on its conduct of the war.

Just the other week, in an extraordinary abandonment of its responsibility, the House, by a decisive margin, defeated the McCloskey resolution which would have required the administration to reveal to it documentation on Laos.

Now this is a most fundamental point. How can one have faith in the system when the House of Representatives votes overwhelmingly to refuse to allow itself to see information on the conduct of a war in which the United States is so deeply involved?

Secondly, there have been recommendations made by several people, including, I believe, Senators Humphrey and Muskie, concerning the establishment of some kind of panel which would have, at least, recommending powers concerning classified information.

I should think that the Congress would want to move rapidly to establish such a panel, but I don't believe it would be appropriate. In fact, I think it would be a waste of time to include Congressmen on the panel because I think there is no surer way of getting such a panel wrapped up in political intrigue and payoffs and accusations than to have members of the Congress from one party deciding that the "in" party's documents should be declassified.

I think that consideration should be given to having persons outside the governmental system compose this body. I would

agree with Senator Muskie that any document more than two years old should be presumed to be declassified.

Perhaps one should go even beyond that. Any document should be *presumed* unclassified unless proof can be brought to bear by the government that it should be classified. The burden of proof to determine declassification or classification should be on the government and not on the panel.

Finally, I think that Congress should make a very serious effort to reinvestigate and come up with firm recommendations on the matter of Executive privilege. If anything has been revealed by the Pentagon Papers, it is that policy decisions for escalation and further involvement were pushed forward by the so-called "crisis managers," none of whom were popularly elected, none of whom were responsible to the Congress. On the other hand, all these men were responsible for keeping Congress and the American people in the dark and for manipulating information to suit their own ends of furthering our involvement.

It is criminal that this situation should be allowed to continue, that the Rostows and the Bundys should have been allowed for so many years to determine and to prearrange American policy without being held responsible to anyone for anything.

It remains criminal that Henry Kissinger should have no other responsibility than the social one of occasionally entertaining a few Congressmen at his pleasure to brief them on any aspect of foreign policy that he decides is fit for print.

In sum, it seems to me that Executive privilege is an area in which Congress may be able and should be able and should want to be able to make inroads.

REP. DOW: You mention the fact that the supporters of the administration shared a common belief system, which I think

is a very descriptive term, indicating that they all viewed the Vietnam situation the same way.

Now I can assure you that almost everybody in Congress did too, so that we had a unanimity, both in the Congress and the Executive branch. We didn't have the benefit of Her Majesty's Loyal Opposition, one of the more useful characteristics of the British Parliamentary system.

We had everybody thinking the same way, without anyone being critical. How did we get that way? Why is it that in a democracy we get to this sort of one-line-of-thinking, one-belief system without any sizable offsetting opposition or criticism? What is the trouble with American democracy? Would anybody care to comment on that?

BISHOP MOORE: I would just like to underline what you are saying and call to our attention that in World War II we were fighting against Fascism and we had Communist allies. Now we find ourselves fighting against Communism with what look like Fascist allies.

To ask your question again, what made the country shift? It is not clear. It seems to me we are up for another shift, and I would like to raise an issue that has already been mentioned. Why is it that we always feel that revolutions around the world are necessarily against our interests? This is another one of those hypotheses that everybody takes for granted. No matter what we do with the system, it will just be a rearrangement unless we challenge the very hypotheses on which the system is now resting.

HON. SEN. GRUENING: There was a very interesting article on the editorial page of the *Washington Post*, July 27, 1971, which implies criticism, not only of the *Post*, but of *The New*

[153]

York Times and other papers which ignored opinions contrary to and critical of United States participation in the war.

For years these newspapers continued to print and promote the administration's propaganda. That was brought home to me when I made the first major speech on the subject on the floor of the Senate on March 10, 1964, calling for the United States to get out of Vietnam. And speaking as an old newspaper man, I knew this was news! When I picked up *The Washington Post* the next morning—and *The New York Times*—expecting to see my speech on the front page, I found it conspicuously missing. Nor was it mentioned in any other part of the papers. *The Columbia Journalism Review* recently devoted an entire issue to an analysis of the failure of the press to cover the war adequately in those days, and it was not so much deliberate, as that the press was not concerned.

The press took the administration's point of view on all of these matters, thus enabling Johnson to campaign on the issue as a peace candidate, on the pledge that he would never send our boys to fight in Asia.

Yet all the time he was making those pledges to the American people, on the basis of which he was swept into office, the Pentagon was maturing plans to do exactly the opposite. This certainly is one of the striking examples of the mendacity that took place in high places. And the press has a certain negative responsibility for not covering these things more fully and inquiring into the motives and into the facts behind them.

I think a vigilant reporter could have found out we were planning to do the very things that Johnson said we were not going to do.

PROF. GURTOV: There is something wrong with a political system that produces individuals who are so like-minded in their perception of world affairs.

There should be much more serious interest in a third-party movement because, as I have tried to suggest, one of the strong impressions one must gain from reading the Pentagon Papers is that it doesn't make any difference which major party happens to be represented in the White House and which is making policy.

More than that, if one looks ahead to the coming election, I for one have very little confidence that the person who might replace Mr. Nixon, based on the most likely possibilities in the Democratic Party, or anyone who may conceivably replace Mr. Nixon as a Republican candidate, is going to compel or precipitate any major turn-around in foreign-policy perspective.

Perhaps another answer is, nobody we can come up with as a third-party candidate—and of course I am not thinking of George Wallace—would be someone representative of real new political movement.

Perhaps such a person, too, is not the kind who can release himself from the shackles of World-War-II thinking. Nevertheless, I am certainly inclined to become much more interested in that alternative.

REP. EDWARDS: I would like to ask Mr. Ellsberg if in addition to the Papers printed in *The New York Times* there were some documents he wished had been published that were not published?

DR. ELLSBERG: I have felt for a couple of years that there really is no substitute for having substantial portions of this material accessible to the citizens and Congress. I felt, from the beginning when I looked at this, it was not a question of a page here and a page there and a collection of sensational secrets.

In fact, I was asked by members of Congress whether I

could give them a list of examples of some fairly dramatic points. I said, "It's not like that." What you have to be able to do is read enough of this in sequence to get a feeling for what is not there at all.

When you see a document here, a document there, you can legitimately say that it is not representative, that there must have been something more sensible, more humane, more concerned that month somewhere else in the files. And you really have to read about three thousand or five thousand pages before you begin to get a very strong sense of confidence, accompanied by a sinking feeling, that such things are not there.

That is the main answer to your question. Secondly, there are individual documents which, if I had been selecting, I would have included, but I don't think that is of major importance. Everyone would choose differently.

However, as journalists have limitations of space, I suppose it may be difficult to give a great deal of space to the earliest periods. I imagine if there were two large sections that I would like to see in print, one would be the entire sweep of intelligence estimates. I think *The New York Times* must have made a decision not to put any of those in, verbatim, but to me the most eye-opening and stunning aspect of the reading was to see how accurate the intelligence estimates, primarily of CIA and State Department analysts, had been over the years. That threw this question of presidential responsibility into a very sharp light and raised many pertinent questions.

The other section would be that which covered the 1945 to 1954 period, including the Geneva Conference. I think that reading had more effect on my own attitudes toward the war and toward the legitimacy of our involvement than any other portions.

So long as we are able to think of this as a civil war that we have wandered into for whatever reasons, we needn't ques-

tion its legitimacy and take comfort in the belief that the United States was simply adding to the burden of a war of the Vietnamese people that would be going on anyway.

To read in some detail the history from 1945 on is to have such an attitude shattered. It certainly worked a very great change in my own thinking, not only about the war but about what the responsibilities were of an American citizen who happened to have this knowledge. So I hope that does come out.

REP. DOW: Do you think, Dr. Ellsberg, that *The Times* had that data available from the 1945 to 1954 period?

DR. ELLSBERG: From what they have published, they had it available.

I can understand the reluctance that many people have to going back that far. In fact, I found over the last few years, even talking to people who had fully authorized access to the material, that to get them to read parts even a year or two earlier than 1961 was difficult because of the attitude: "That is past history and is no longer relevant."

I understand the attitude. I didn't read the earlier part myself until the very last. I went backward in fact. What I found was that year by year my perception of the war changed kaleidoscopically as I peeled off one year after another of American involvement.

What the Papers reveal about the 1945 and 1950 period, I found staggering. I think *The New York Times* felt that with a limited amount of space they had to concentrate on the more dramatic and more recent material. But I do hope that Congressmen and citizens will really take the effort to read that earlier part of the Papers.

[1 5 7]

MR. RASKIN: I would like to say something again about the situation at the end of the Second World War and see where that brings us in terms of the present.

The Pentagon Papers show us how a group of men undertake to manage an empire. They show how there was no end to which they would not go in pursuit of their particular objectives, so long as they remained within the limits of avoiding a nuclear war.

And indeed, from time to time, even that "option" seemed to be something they were prepared to think about seriously. What we have seen among our elite is a group of people purportedly acting in the name of society, who arrogated much to themselves, pretty much going their own particular way without reference to anyone but themselves.

They were interested in creating a reality: that of domination in Southeast Asia at whatever the cost. It is that reason —their belief that Indochina could become like middle-class suburbs, or barring that, a Watts—which resulted in no attention being paid to facts or accurate intelligence estimates.

Secretary Rusk has said: "The problem with Americans is that they do not like the imperial game." [4] As he pointed out to one historian: "Scratch the skin of any American and you find he wants to take care of his own affairs and not get involved. There is no imperium in Americans, at least not in the postwar period. Acts of will since World War II have not erased the institution of isolationism." [5]

I take it that what he is referring to when he talks about acts of will are the attempts on the part of various people within the Executive and the establishment, parts of the bureaucracy, to institutionalize American activities around the

[4] *The Tuesday Cabinet* by Henry P. Graff. Englewood Cliffs, N.J.: Prentice-Hall, 1970.
[5] Ibid., p. 135.

world, either through a base structure, covert operations in different places or in war-making of the kind that occurred in Indochina.

But now, having uncovered the face of imperialism, where do we go from here? At the end of the Second World War, at least part of the American government felt very strongly, and indeed it was, as General Telford Taylor has pointed out, the position of the American government itself, that militarism, imperialism and ultranationalism were illegal.

And as Joseph Keenan, the American prosecutor at the Tokyo trials, said when he prosecuted the leaders of the Japanese at that period: "It may seem strange to include charges of murder in an indictment before an international tribunal, but it is high time and indeed [it] was there before this war began, that the promoters of aggressive, ruthless war and treaty-breakers should be stripped of being national heroes and exposed for what they are: plain ordinary murderers." [6]

Between 1945 and 1947, the United States, pursuing the ideal that there had to be new international laws which would stop war crimes and stop aggressive war, took the leadership in saying that there should be standards in the world, international standards, which could then be adopted by particular nations, including the United States. I think we are now beginning, if somewhat belatedly, to come back to such an objective. What we are talking about, as one studies the Pentagon Papers, is the question of the waging of an aggressive war. It is not enough to go merely down the command line saying that the sergeants and lieutenants have to share the responsibility for what goes on. Indeed, it is the people at the top of the government who must accept that responsibility. The elite who manufactured the war, manufactured institutional structures to carry out that war and did so with the acts of will that Secretary Rusk spoke about, cannot assume that

[6] Department of State Bulletin, May 19, 1946, pp. 846–847.

they are going to be praised forever as the brightest and the best.

What one learns from history can always be somewhat deceptive.

I suppose the real lesson of the Second World War and Vietnam was Nuremburg, not Munich. In Germany, a group of people, supported to be sure by the largest military and economic institutions, spearheaded the Second World War. This group was adjudged to be beyond the pale of politics because they had turned the state into a criminal enterprise. The lesson of Nuremberg was to guard against such groups. In the United States another group thought that politics and the state meant criminal activity. They initiated and supported a disastrous war which pulled American society into the nest of misery.

Unless we come to grips with understanding the events of the last generation, there is no reason to believe, first, that the war will not continue in one form or another, and second, that the same habits of mind, that is, the imperial habits of mind and the institutional structures which led to the war in Vietnam will not in fact, be operative in other places, whether in Bolivia or Thailand or wherever.

In my view, the war itself will not stop until it is perfectly clear that there is a change in the value system of the country. Our order of priorities cannot change until a different sort of value system comes into play. In other words, it is dubious whether those whose values favored the war—if it could have been won—will ever clearly see the needs of the American society. Their priorities will always be flawed because of their dreams of empire.

The irony is that the very people who were correct on these matters will find themselves barred from participating in the government of the United States. They will find themselves excluded from positions of national security and foreign policy.

So we are in a situation now, in my view, where what we have to do is re-examine our own value system, but more important for the Congress, a system of saying there must be some code of behavior by which public officials in the United States holding high office—whether they are Assistant Secretaries of State or GS 18's or whatever—are to be held accountable. Unless individuals in the government understand that they can be held to account, just as Lieutenant Calley was held to account, we will find that civilians who are, in fact, penny-ante militarists will continue to set the stage for exactly this sort of war in other places.

I would also argue that some sort of sanctions apply to the individuals directly or indirectly involved in making the war. The Democratic Party, for example, might take the position that all such individuals should be barred from office for at least ten years from the time they left the government.

We ought to establish a uniform code of justice for public officials whose responsibilities include but are not limited to the foreign and national security policies of the United States.

The first section of the code would make clear the kind of things that people in power—bureaucrats, policy makers—could not do, such as planning and carrying out plans for mass defoliation, deportations, brutality against civilians and insurgent groups, pillages and mass bombings.

As a case in point, the establishment of concentration camps, labor camps and detention camps, or the undertaking of covert military moves by government officials, which some people believe constituted the beginning of the Vietnam war must now be considered proscribed activity on the part of United States government officials. Such a proscription flows from our own directives on German and Japanese society as well as international law.

Then to develop from the various international laws that

have been laid down since 1899 activities from which, in fact, leaders and states would be barred.

From that, we set out penalties for the planning, ordering and carrying out of such action, which individual penalties would apply to government officials.

We should develop two legal offices. One would be a legal office of the president which would deal with national security affairs. That particular office would have to pass on the legality, according to international and domestic law, of various governmental actions, using as a guide the Uniform Code of Military Justice, the Nuremberg and Asian war-crime trials and directives laid on Japan and Germany and Austria by the United States during the period 1945 to 1947.

In addition, we should establish a court of international law and security to hear cases from citizens who may be aware of such matters both within the United States and outside it.

There should be a national security legal adviser, equal in status to a Parliamentarian for the House or Senate. He would analyze the various bills that came through committee and be available for advice to Congressmen and Senators so they could be sure that their actions were in line with international law and with the various United Nations Charter and Assembly resolutions.

Beyond that, there should be a jury system to oversee and operate within the government itself to be sure that the national security legal officers were in fact analyzing various programs laid before the President and the national security bureaucracy.

Violations of judicial decisions should be subject to impeachment proceedings. Indeed cases could be brought before federal courts for people not to pay their taxes and for people of draft age not to have to serve in the armed forces.

So, in effect, you have a triple level of involvement. At the

first level you would establish a law. The second level would bring into operation a new legal system to oversee national security and foreign-policy affairs. The third level would insure that when the courts could not get the government to accept their injunctions, the people themselves would have the right of taking into the courts the decisions not to pay taxes or to redirect their taxes away from the federal government.

I would see this as the only real way and, by the same token, a very tough way, of attempting to stop the continued degradation of government processes. We would be setting a new standard of government, which in fact was imposed on other societies by the United States a generation ago.

MR. KOWALSKI: I have not had an opportunity to study your proposal so I hesitate to comment. Certainly, if society can legislate against corruption and bribery in government, it should be able to condemn and outlaw those who plan criminal war and carry the nation into senseless immoral bombing of people who have done nothing to us and whom we do not know.

Documents coming to light on the war in Southeast Asia clearly show that upstanding citizens, so-called respected leaders of the country, have been engaged in planning criminal operations. They try to excuse their actions as only contingency planning; but whether the plans were executed or not, there is no question that the insidious proposals were criminal designs against humanity. I suppose the ideal solution would be to have a world code.

It would seem to me that the code would be most difficult to write so that it did not prevent or hamper our military in the execution of their legitimate defense functions.

What will your code say, Mr. Raskin, about nuclear weapons? We dropped two atom bombs on Japan because Ja-

pan didn't have one to retaliate with. We have a deadly standoff today because a nuclear exchange would be suicidal. But we have this standoff precisely because planning for use of nuclear weapons goes on endlessly in the military. How do you formulate a code to answer this problem?

MR. RASKIN: I think there are several ways. First of all, it may very well be the case that we are going to have to give up the idea of nuclear weapons as a principle; but beyond that, I would see this code as applying, at this stage, to civilians.

In terms of nuclear weapons generally, I would say that the use of weapons of mass destruction should now be debated in the context of criminality. Indeed, the fact that the genocide treaty has passed the Senate Foreign Relations Committee and may be passed by the Senate itself, twenty-three years after it was first introduced, will cause a reconsideration of that entire question.

There may not necessarily be an intent to destroy a group, but the reality is that with the use of nuclear weapons, you indeed destroy whole societies, and the intent to destroy a particular society can be adduced from the plans themselves.

I would argue that once the genocide treaty is passed by the Senate itself, that if the treaty is not executed, a new law will have to be formulated to make the employment of nuclear weapons criminal.

What I have done is list eleven different areas where such plans and policies would have to be proscribed, such as assassination of other leaders within the United States, mass bombing and undeclared aggressive war, the use of weapons—such as nuclear weapons of whatever kilotonnage or megatonnage —of mass destruction.

Also proscribed would be weapons declared illegal under the Hague Conventions of 1899–1907, agreements with corpo-

rate or other leaderships for the purpose of making war, the threatening and provoking of other nations and lands with United States or third party military forces. I propose the use of legal limitations to demilitarize American foreign policy. I would say these are exactly the terms that the United States used in Germany, Japan and Austria, where it attempted to set forth a legal code using international law and various sorts of resolutions passed in the House and Senate as the basis of demilitarizing other societies.

To a great extent this attempt at demilitarization failed because it was the sword's point for imperialism in another land. But the question now is different. How do we set a legal code to work in demilitarizing our own society and, more specifically, our own government?

It is within that context, I would argue, that you cause a value change, a mind change, in society which could finally bring us to a point where individuals and government know that such wars are no longer the meaning of statecraft.

MR. KOWALSKI: I have a deep feeling for the military because I served with them so long. Accordingly, I wonder, would there be a place in your code for a bill of rights for military officers?

Specifically, many of them are called upon to speak on political problems in support of the administration. Officers have been used by administrations to ballyhoo war, support the draft and propagandize the nation on weapons systems. These are all political matters.

I would like to see, in your code, a bill of rights for the Army officer or military officer, with provisions that he could not be called upon by any administration to support a political point of view.

There are other areas where a code might be helpful to the

military. For example, military officers have in the past had to support certain manufacturing establishments. The excuse given by civilian superiors has been that the plant or company was essential to the defense of the United States. Military officers should have the right to resist this manipulation. And I might add, if they don't, the code should hold them accountable.

MR. RASKIN: My guess is that one of the results of the demoralization of the Army because of the Indochina war is the need to develop new rules of law for the military itself. I think this is a very important issue and should be extended not only to officers but to enlisted men in the armed forces, in the sense that we begin to reconstitute how a peaceful nation should view the role of the military.

PROF. GURTOV: In criticizing those responsible for our involvement in Southeast Asia, it is not important that particular members of an administration, who are shown in a very bad light by the Pentagon Papers, supported certain positions in the government. What is important is their extraordinary hard-headedness and their absolute refusal to deal with counterevidence. This is what strikes me as most inviting of blame.

MR. RASKIN: Why do you think they did not want to deal with counterevidence?

PROF. GURTOV: This is certainly a key question. Perhaps it calls for some measure of psychoanalysis since there is a psychological dimension to decision making and decision makers.

Certainly one can argue that they shared a very basic assumption about the way the world is structured and about American responsibilities in that world. But I am not sure that

[166]

really is the answer to why people hold to certain views. Perhaps the answer is that once they make certain commitments in support of those views, they find it impossible to turn around and start looking at basic assumptions.

Of course, that is why we find that throughout the Pentagon Papers there are very few instances in which anyone wanted to examine the basic assumptions, even though there were clearly opportunities for such questioning.

MR. RASKIN: To what extent would the existence of a code cause dissonance in the habits and minds of bureaucrats so that they at least be forced to say; maybe we shouldn't do this, or we better not do this, or we better look at alternatives because this is proscribed? In other words, to what extent is their habit of mind set because there is no input, so to speak, from any other value system which would allow an alternative way of carrying out policy?

PROF. GURTOV: I question whether a code would be worth the effort, because it is, after all, a matter of the individuals, and a code is not going to remake the individual.

It seems to me that if you are faced with the kinds of people who made policy in the 1950's, 1960's and early 1970's, if there were such a code as you have proposed, I tend to think that the devious and perverted intelligence that is characteristic of these men would be looking for ways around that code. Perhaps this is because I am at the height of my pessimism. I am not saying that such a code is not worthwhile, but it does take a good man to make a good code.

MR. RASKIN: There is very little in what you say that I would disagree with. I think the problem though is that what you are describing is, in fact, revolution.

[167]

In other words, what you are saying is there is no way around this ruling elite, which is in some sense setting a behavioral term of reference. I would suggest there has to be a middle course. And that middle course is, first of all, to offer standards, certainly for younger people who come into these bureaucracies.

Secondly, in the service of that middle course, the Congress can reassert itself and say, we are now going to see certain behavior as criminal and we are going to ban that behavior as criminal; and we are going to make it known in society that that is the case, and whoever is in power is going to have to accept this legal code.

At the very least, what it does, I would argue, is set a stage for the value change in society, as, for example, did the civil-rights laws. While it is true that the poor have not benefited very much in civil rights over the last decade, the laws have led to changes in societal attitudes which differ sharply from those existing prior to the 1954 period.

So I think we can at least talk in terms of what the Congress is able to do in that direction and within that framework.

REP. RYAN: Even if the higher echelons find various ways to circumvent the code, is it not possible that the existence of a code would be more likely to guide staff people at the staff level?

It also might inhibit them from carrying out some of the decisions of the policy makers and stimulate from within the kind of dissent which might bring about a change in policy. During the period to which the Pentagon Papers are addressed, disagreement or dissent on policy, to the extent it existed, was never exposed.

PROF. MARR: I strongly question whether such a code in the 1950's and 1960's when the Pentagon Papers were being written would have been any good at all, the most fundamental point being that laws don't really produce value change but rather vice versa.

In some ways, and I hesitate to use historical parallels, Mr. Raskin is bringing up the old arguments between the Second International and the Third International prior to World War I, taking the position of the Second International apropos of how to remake the system and reform it from the inside.

I think we face a much more current and imminent crisis, one facet of which is the ending of the Vietnam war. That is what I am interested in. I don't think we should devote our time to structural reform of Congress and legal restrictions on bureaucrats to prevent future wars until we have stopped this war we are in right now.

Crowd scene from Congressional Conference on Pentagon Papers

Left to right—lower tier: Rep. Drinan, Rep. Eckhardt, Anthony
Russo, Rep. Helstoski, Melvin Gurtov, Fred Branfman, Rep. Koch,
Rep. Dow, Ernest Gruening and Gen. Thi. *Left to right—upper tier:*
Rep. Burton, Rep. Abourezk, Rep. Mikva and Rep. Kastenmeier

Left to right: David Truong, Rep. Drinan, Rep. Eckhardt and Anthony Russo

Left to right: Fred Branfman, Rep. Koch, Rep. Dow, Ernest Gruening, Gen. Thi *(blocked by Gruening),* Noam Chomsky, Tran Van Dinh, Cynthia Fredrick

Left to right: Rep. Rosenthal *(striped shirt),* Anthony Russo, Rep. Helstoski, Melvin Gurtov, Fred Branfman, Rep. Koch *(standing)* and Rep. Dow

Left to right: Rep. Dow, Ernest Gruening, Gen. Thi and Rep. Ryan

Left to right: Rep. Koch, Rep. Kastenmeier, Ernest Gruening and Gen. Thi

Left to right: Tran Van Dinh, Cynthia Fredrick, Ngo Vinh Long and David Marr

Left to right: Ernest Gruening, Rep. Dow, Rep. Koch and Fred Branfman

Left to right: Rep. Abourezk, Rep. Mikva

Rep. Abourezk

Profiles of Contributors to the Congressional Conference on the Pentagon Papers July 27–29, 1971

*JAMES G. ABOUREZK of Rapid City, South Dakota, was elected to his first term in the United States House of Representatives in November of 1970. He serves on both the House Interior and Insular Affairs Committee and the House Judiciary Committee. Prior to his election, he practiced law in Rapid City. He has been admitted to practice before the South Dakota Supreme Court, the Federal District Court of South Dakota, and the United States Supreme Court. Before coming to Congress he was active in South Dakota in the areas of mental health, community action, consumer affairs and the legal aid program. He is currently a candidate for the United States Senate from South Dakota.

*PHILLIP BURTON is chairman of the Democratic Study Group, an organization composed of some 160 liberal Members of the House of Representatives. At the 1968 Democratic convention, Congressman Burton led the fight to place a strong Vietnam peace plank in the platform. Since his election to Congress from San Francisco in 1964, he has been one of a small number of Members who have consistently voted against American military involvement in Southeast Asia. He has been active in reforming the procedures of the House both as

---

House members who have been marked with an asterisk (*) were sponsors of this conference.

[1 7 7]

a Member of the Democratic Reform Committee, which revised the seniority system, and of its successor, the Committee on Organization, Study and Review, which continues to work for further improvements. He is chairman of the House Interior Committee's Subcommittee on Territories and has sponsored legislation extending self-government to America's overseas possessions. He is a Member of the House Education and Labor Committee and is considered one of the House's leading experts on social insurance, health care and public assistance. He was author of the black lung compensation provisions of the Coal Mine Health and Safety Act and is responsible for bringing millions of additional workers under the protection of minimum wage laws. During most of his forty-five years, Congressman Burton has been active in public affairs and served as a member of the California State Legislature for eight years.

FRED BRANFMAN is currently director of Project Air War, a nonprofit organization aimed at raising public consciousness about the air war in Indochina. A branch of the Indochina Education Council, Project Air War is located in Washington, D.C. Project materials have appeared in *The New York Times*, *Time* magazine, *The Washington Post*, *Congressional Record* and numerous other publications, and have been displayed on the Walter Cronkite CBS news program. Fred Branfman spent four years in Laos, from March 1967 until February of 1971. He spent his first two years as a volunteer with International Voluntary Services, Inc., (IVS), a nonprofit organization contracted to the Agency for International Development. As a volunteer, he learned to speak Laotian and French. His final two years in Laos were spent doing research, writing, interpreting, and working as a free-lance contributor to Dispatch News Service International. During this period he interviewed several thousand refugees from American bombing; dozens of

American pilots and air-war officials; and local government and embassy officials in Laos, South Vietnam, Thailand and Cambodia. A part of this experience is summed up in "The Presidential War in Laos: 1964–1970," published in *Laos: War and Revolution*. His latest book, *Voices From the Plain of Jars*, will be published in 1972 by Harper and Row.

NOAM CHOMSKY is Ferrari P. Ward Professor of linguistics at the Massachusetts Institute of Technology, where he has been on the academic staff since 1955. He is the author of books and articles on linguistics, philosophy of language, intellectual history and contemporary affairs. The most recent books are *American Power and the New Mandarins*, *At War With Asia* and *Problems of Knowledge and Freedom: the Russell Lectures.*

*JOHN CONYERS, JR., of Detroit, Michigan, was elected to his fourth term in the U.S. House of Representatives in 1970 with eighty-eight per cent of the vote. He is a member of the House Judiciary Committee and Government Operations Committee. He authored the only amendment passed by the House which strengthened the Fair Housing section of the 1966 Civil Rights bill. Congressman Conyers organized three fact-finding missions by Congressmen to Alabama and Mississippi to investigate violations of civil and voting rights. In the spring of 1969 he toured Vietnam as part of a United States Study Team investigating religious and political freedoms. He is Vice Chairman of the national board of Americans for Democratic Action, Vice Chairman of Advisory Council, American Civil Liberties Union, and belongs to Members of Congress for Peace through Law. In 1967 he received the Rosa Parks Award for civil rights activities from the Southern Christian Leadership Conference. In the House, he is the

[179]

sponsor of the Full Opportunity Act, which would provide thirty billion dollars yearly for a ten-year period to aid low income Americans in the areas of jobs, housing and education. He has also sponsored legislation to make January 15, Martin Luther King's birthday, a national holiday.

TRAN VAN DINH, a former Minister Plenipotentiary of the South Vietnamese Foreign Service and a former cabinet member of the Ngo Dinh Diem administration, is now Professor of Asian Studies at the Afro-Asian Institute, Temple University, Philadelphia, Pennsylvania.

*JOHN G. Dow from Newburgh, New York, was elected to Congress in 1964 and serves on the House Agriculture Committee where he has taken strong positions for protection of the environment. In 1965, Congressman Dow was one of the seven Representatives to vote against the first appropriation bill containing funds for the Vietnam war. He was the only member of the House to be sent in 1967 at the expense of his constituents, on a fact-finding tour of Vietnam, where he spent eight days, Hong Kong, Thailand and Laos. At the 1968 Democratic National Convention, Mr. Dow spoke on behalf of the minority plank on Vietnam. Congressman Dow has actively promoted legislation to benefit the elderly, and is known as a strong civil rights supporter. An outspoken conservationist, he was the first House Member to use recycled paper in his office and has introduced legislation to require its use by the federal government. In 1971 Mr. Dow was the chairman of the Congressional Conference on the Pentagon Papers, on which this book is based. Before coming to Congress, Mr. Dow was a business systems analyst for a number of large corporations dealing in such diverse products as foods, drugs, aircraft parts and railroad equipment as well as in banking

and advertising services. During World War II he served on an industry-wide committee to expedite munitions shipments.

*ROBERT FREDERICK DRINAN was first elected to Congress from Massachusetts in November of 1970. He serves on the House Judiciary Committee and on the House Internal Security Committee. A Jesuit, Congressman Drinan was ordained in 1953. A graduate of Georgetown University Law Center, he was admitted to the D.C. bar in 1950, the Massachusetts bar in 1956 and admitted to practice before the Supreme Court in 1955. From 1955–1956 he was the Assistant Dean of Boston College Law School and served as Dean from 1956 until 1970. From 1962 until 1970, he served as the chairman of the Advisory Committee for Massachusetts to the U.S. Commission on Civil Rights. He has been a member of the executive committee of the Association of American Law Schools; he was elected as a Fellow at the American Academy of Arts and Sciences and is a member of the American, Massachusetts and Boston bar associations and a member of the American Law Institute. Congressman Drinan was a corresponding editor for *America,* a national Catholic weekly from 1958–1970 and is the author of three books: *Religion, The Courts and Public Policy,* 1963; *Democracy, Dissent & Disorder,* 1969; and *Vietnam and Armageddon,* 1970. He has received Honorary Doctor of Laws degrees from Worcester State College, Long Island University, and Rhode Island College.

*BOB ECKHARDT of Houston, Texas, was elected to the United States House of Representatives in 1966. He serves as a Member of the Subcommittee on Commerce and Finance of the Interstate and Foreign Commerce Committee. Eckhardt was among the first Congressmen to express concern about the

scale and direction of our nation's involvement in Vietnam. His long-time interest in consumer protection has resulted in his origination and introduction of the Consumer Class Action Bill and a comprehensive no-fault auto insurance bill. Known for his concern with the rights of man and the upholding of constitutionally granted liberties, Congressman Eckhardt was an active opponent of the restrictive and constitutionally questionable provisions of the recently passed Drug Abuse Act and Organized Crime Bill. Eckhardt, on behalf of twenty-six Members of Congress, presented arguments in the United States District Court, the Court of Appeals and the Supreme Court in support of the publication of the Pentagon Papers. Prior to his election to Congress, he practiced law in Texas and was a member of the Texas House of Representatives representing Harris County (Houston) from 1958 until 1966.

*Don Edwards, Democrat of San Jose, California, was first elected to the United States House of Representatives in November of 1962. He is a Member of the House Judiciary Committee and is chairman of that committee's Civil Rights Subcommittee. Mr. Edwards' subcommittee also has exclusive jurisdiction over bankruptcy, certain consumer matters, federal holidays and constitutional amendments such as the Equal Rights for Men and Women amendment. Congressman Edwards is also a Member of the Veterans' Affairs Committee where he serves on the Education and Training, and Hospital subcommittees. Articles by Congressman Edwards have appeared in *The Progressive, Agenda, Trial* and other periodicals. A member of the California State Bar Association, Mr. Edwards was admitted to practice before the United States Supreme Court in 1964. In 1967–1969 he served on the National Commission on Reform of Federal Criminal Laws and is now serving on the President's Commission on the Bank-

ruptcy Laws of the United States. A former FBI agent, he served as a Naval Intelligence Officer during World War II, and volunteered for sea duty as a Naval Gunnery Officer. He was a San Jose businessman when first elected to the 88th Congress.

DANIEL ELLSBERG is a Senior Research Associate of the Center for International Studies at Massachusetts Institute of Technology. From 1967 until April, 1970, he was a Vietnam analyst for the Rand Corporation in Santa Monica, California. He is a graduate of Harvard University with a Ph.D. in economics. In 1964 and 1965 he was special assistant to the Assistant Secretary of Defense for International Security Affairs, working on Vietnam affairs. He joined the State Department in 1965 to go to Vietnam as a member of General Edward G. Lansdale's liaison office. From December, 1966, to June, 1967, he was special assistant to the Deputy U.S. Ambassador in Vietnam, with responsibility for evaluating pacification. In June of 1971 he took responsibility for making public the heretofore secret Pentagon Papers.

*DONALD M. FRASER was elected in 1962 to represent Minneapolis, Minnesota, in the United States House of Representatives. He serves as chairman of the House Foreign Affairs Subcommittee on International Organizations and Movements, and is a member of three other subcommittees, National Security Policy and Scientific Developments, Foreign Economic Policy and State Department Organization and Foreign Operations. He is also a member of the House District of Columbia Committee. Congressman Fraser, a past chairman of the Democratic Study Group, has belonged to Members of Congress for Peace Through Law since 1963. In 1964 he organized and

[183]

became the first American co-chairman of the Anglo-American Parliamentary Conference on Africa and currently is a participating member in the Conference. Mr. Fraser is the author of Title IX of the Foreign Assistance Act, which calls for increased emphasis on building democratic institutions in underdeveloped nations. He is presently the chairman of the Democratic Party's Commission on Party Structure and Delegate Selection. A Minneapolis attorney prior to his election to Congress, he served in the Minnesota State Senate from 1955 through 1962, and sponsored legislation in the fields of education, taxation, fair housing, municipal affairs and constitutional law.

CYNTHIA FREDRICK was in Vietnam from the spring of 1966 through the spring of 1967 doing research on her Ph.D. With the completion of her thesis, "The South Vietnamese Constitution of April 1, 1967: The Institutionalization of Politics in the Second Republic," she received her doctorate from the University of London's School of Oriental and African Studies in 1969. From 1969 until 1970 she did post-doctoral work at Harvard University in Far Eastern studies. She is currently the east coast coordinator of the Committee of Concerned Asian Scholars and is coordinating the Cambridge-Goddard Graduate School of Social Change in Cambridge, Massachusetts, where she is also teaching a course on revolution in Southeast Asia.

ERNEST GRUENING served Alaska in the United States Senate from 1959 until 1969. In 1964 he was one of two senators who voted against the Gulf of Tonkin resolution. Hon. Senator Gruening, who graduated from Harvard Medical School in 1912, left medicine to become a journalist. His newspaper career began in Boston as the managing editor of *The Boston*

Traveler from 1914 to 1916. From 1916–1918 he was managing editor of *The Boston Journal;* managing editor of *The New York Tribune,* 1918; managing editor of *The Nation,* 1920–1923; and editor of *The Portland Evening News* from 1927 until 1933. In 1934 he was appointed director of the Division of Territories and Island Possessions of the Department, serving in that capacity until 1939. In the same year he was appointed governor of Alaska, was twice reappointed, and served until 1953. He is the author of a number of books, including *The Public Pays* and *The Battle for Alaskan Statehood.*

MELVIN GURTOV is associate professor of political science at the University of California, Riverside. Previously, he was, from August 1966 to June 1971, a member of the social science department of the Rand Corporation. In the summer of 1967 he joined the first group of analysts which worked in Washington on the Pentagon Papers. A specialist on China and Southeast Asia, Dr. Gurtov's books include: *The First Vietnam Crisis* (Columbia University Press, 1967); *Southeast Asia Tomorrow: Problems and Prospects for U.S. Policy* (Johns Hopkins Press, 1970); and *China and Southeast Asia—the Politics of Survival* (D.C. Heath, 1971).

MORTON H. HALPERIN joined the Brookings Institution in September, 1969, to work on a book on bureaucratic politics and foreign policy. He is a Senior Fellow associated with the Foreign Policy Division of Brookings. Previously Mr. Halperin served for more than three years in the federal government. Most recently he was a senior staff member of the National Security Council Staff with responsibility for National Security Council planning. Before moving to the White House at the start of the Nixon administration, Mr. Halperin was a Deputy

Assistant Secretary of Defense in the Office of the Assistant Secretary of Defense (International Security Affairs). He was responsible for political-military planning and for matters of arms control and disarmament. Mr. Halperin joined the Defense Department in 1966 as Special Assistant for Planning to the then Assistant Secretary of Defense, John McNaughton. Prior to that time, Mr. Halperin was associated for six years with Harvard University where he was an Assistant Professor of Government and a Research Associate of the Harvard Center for International Affairs. He is the author of *Defense Strategies for the Seventies* and *Limited War in the Nuclear Age;* he is co-author of *Strategy and Arms Control* and *Communist China and Arms Control.* He is a member of the Council on Foreign Relations and the Institute for Strategic Studies.

*MICHAEL HARRINGTON, elected to Congress from Massachusetts in a special election in 1969, serves on the House Armed Services Committee. As a committee member, Harrington has questioned the policy of flooding the military with more money than it needs at a time when domestic programs suffer from large budget cuts because they are considered inflationary by some. He was one of the leaders in the successful effort to pass the House Reorganization Act of 1970, the first reorganization bill to succeed in twenty years. Before the bill was passed, some congressmen relished their anonymity and hid behind a system which allowed their votes on controversial issues to remain secret. Now, their votes are on the record, making it possible for their constituents to vote on their congressmen's actual record and not the image of that record. Harrington left the private sector for public affairs early in life, running for Salem City Council in 1959, just a year after he graduated from Harvard with honors in history. Only twenty-four years old at the time, and a student at Harvard

Law School, Harrington won his first election and served for three years before he ran for mayor and lost in 1963. In 1964 he won a seat in the legislature and was re-elected twice. In 1967 he was elected Democratic State Committeeman, a job which he currently holds.

*HENRY HELSTOSKI was elected to Congress in 1964 to represent the Ninth Congressional District of New Jersey and thus end the twenty-six year Republican incumbency in the office. He is a member of the House Interstate and Foreign Commerce Committee and the House Committee on Veterans' Affairs. With a background in administration and in social studies, from 1949 to 1962 he was an educator serving in the capacities of teacher, department head, principal, and superintendent in schools at East Rutherford, Cedar Grove and Wallington, New Jersey. In 1956 at the age of thirty he was elected a councilman in East Rutherford. The following year he was elected Mayor of East Rutherford and served for eight years until his election to the Congress. Additionally, his years of public service included: chairman, for eight years of the Joint Sewer Authority of Rutherford, East Rutherford and Carlstadt; member of the executive committee of Meadowland Regional Development Agency, made up of thirteen municipalities; member of the Bergen County Mental Health Board; and organizer and member of the Regional Air Pollution Council, an organization of local officials in New Jersey.

DOUG HOSTETTER, after graduation in 1966 from Eastern Mennonite College, volunteered for a three-year tour as teacher and community development worker in Vietnam with the Mennonite Central Committee. During his three years in the village of Tam Ky—a heavy combat zone about forty miles

[187]

south of Danang—he was able to set up a crafts project which supported fifty families, sewing classes in five refugee camps and a literacy program which used high school students to teach over five thousand Vietnamese children how to read and write their own language. In addition he spent part of the time teaching English in the local high schools and setting up literacy and tailoring classes in the local political prisons. Because of his fluency in Vietnamese, Mr. Hostetter accompanied a National Student Association delegation of student body presidents and college newspaper editors which traveled to Saigon and Hanoi in December of 1970 to negotiate the People's Peace Treaty. He was the first Vietnamese-speaking American to be allowed to travel in Hanoi since 1954. He is currently working as Research Coordinator for Vietnam and China under the United Methodist Office for the United Nations.

*ROBERT W. KASTENMEIER, first elected to Congress from Wisconsin in November of 1958, presently is chairman of the House Judiciary Committee's Subcommittee on Correction and Revision of Laws. Most recently his subcommittee has held hearings around the country on the subject of prison reform. He is also a member of the House Committee on Interior and Insular Affairs and serves on four subcommittees: Environment, National Parks and Recreation, Mining, and Public Lands. In 1965 Congressman Kastenmeier was the first Member of Congress to hold hearings in his district on the Vietnam war and consequently published *Hearings on Vietnam: Voices from the Grassroots.* He received his law degree from the University of Wisconsin and was subsequently admitted to practice in Wisconsin, and before the United States District Court and the United States Supreme Court. From 1955–1958 he was elected Justice of the Peace for Dodge and Jefferson Counties in Wisconsin.

*EDWARD I. KOCH was elected to Congress from New York City in November of 1968. As a member of the House Banking and Currency Committee, he serves on three subcommittees: Consumer Affairs, Bank Supervision and Insurance, and International Trade. An outspoken opponent of the Vietnam War, in May of 1969 Representative Koch introduced one of the first resolutions calling for the withdrawal of American troops and has consistently voted against appropriations for the further prosecution of the Vietnam War. He is the principal sponsor of legislation to provide for selective conscientious objector status in the draft; this year he introduced the first bill to provide conditional amnesty for draft resisters. Rep. Koch first made political news in 1963 when he defeated, in an upset, former Tammany Hall Leader Carmine De Sapio for Democratic District Leader in Greenwich Village. Since then Mr. Koch has continued to beat the political odds. In 1966 he was elected to the City Council, as the first Democrat in thirty-eight years to represent Manhattan's second Councilmanic District. In 1968 he became the first Democrat in thirty-one years to represent the 17th Congressional District (The Silk Stocking district) in Congress. Upon his election, Mr. Koch discontinued his law practice to devote all his energy to his Congressional duties.

FRANK KOWALSKI, a retired colonel in the United States Army, served in Congress from 1958 to 1962 as a Representative from Connecticut. He is a graduate of the United States Military Academy at West Point and did graduate work at the Massachusetts Institute of Technology and Columbia University. During his Army career he was director of a program for disarmament of Germany, chief of staff of the United States Advisory group in Japan and commandant of the United States Army Command Management School. While in Con-

gress he served on the House Armed Services Committee. He was a member of the Subversive Activities Control Board from 1963 to 1967. He is the author of *Rearmament of Japan,* published in 1969.

NGO VINH LONG is a citizen of South Vietnam, who is presently a Ph.D. candidate in East Asian Studies at Harvard University, specializing on Vietnam. He recently founded the Vietnam Resource Center in Boston. Mr. Long is the editor of "Thoi Bao Ga," a bi-monthly newsletter by Vietnamese writers and is the author of a forthcoming book to be published by Harvard entitled: *Before the August Revolution: The Living Conditions of the Vietnamese Peasants Under the French.*

DON LUCE went to Vietnam in 1958 as an agricultural volunteer with International Voluntary Services (IVS). From 1961 to 1967 he was the Vietnam director of IVS. He spent 1968 at Cornell University as a research associate at the Center for International Studies. From October 1968 to May 1971 Mr. Luce worked in Vietnam as a journalist and a research associate on postwar reconstruction for the World Council of Churches. He was asked to leave Vietnam in May 1971 by the South Vietnamese government because of his role in exposing the "Tiger Cages" of Con Son Island prison. He is co-author of *Viet Nam: The Unheard Voices.* At present, he is touring the United States with a mobile exhibit of photographs, art and artifacts of the people of Indochina. This Mobile Education Project, aimed at educating Americans about the Indochinese, is a program sponsored by the Indochina Education Council in Washington, D.C.

DAVID G. MARR, a visiting assistant professor of Vietnamese Studies at Cornell University, is co-director of the Indochina

Resource Center, a branch of the Indochina Education Council located in Washington, D.C. He recently returned from a four-month trip to Paris, where he carried out research on contemporary Vietnam under a grant from the National Endowment for Humanities. During his stay there, he published a number of articles—based on his Paris contacts—about the Paris Peace Talks. He is the author of *Vietnamese Anticolonialism, 1885–1925)* (University of California Press, 1971). Professor Marr, a member of the Committee of Concerned Asian Scholars, did his M.A. research on political attitudes and activities of young urban intellectuals in Vietnam in 1965. His Ph.D. research on Vietnam's anticolonial movements, 1885–1925, was done in Vietnam in 1967. Both degrees were obtained at the University of California, Berkeley.

*ABNER J. MIKVA of Illinois is serving his second term in Congress. He is a member of the House Committees on the Judiciary and the District of Columbia, a vice-chairman of the Democratic Study Group and national vice-chairman of Americans for Democratic Action. In his four years in Congress, he has been a leader in the efforts to enfranchise eighteen-year-old voters, protect civil rights and liberties and reduce military spending and waste. Congressman Mikva served on the National Commission on Reform of Federal Criminal Laws and has been appointed to the National Commission on Individual Rights. Mikva, who is forty-six, served five terms in the Illinois House of Representatives where he was chairman of the House Judiciary Committee. He was the first to sponsor a comprehensive Code of Ethics for state officials. He also sponsored Illinois' new Criminal Code, a model for the country, and successfully proposed important legislation in the fields of civil rights and mental health. Congressman Mikva has been the recipient of the Page One Award from the Chicago News-

paper Guild for his "outstanding contribution to a better Chicago" and received several "Best Legislator" awards from the Independent Voters of Illinois. He was graduated cum laude from the University of Chicago Law School in 1951 where he was editor of the Law Review and elected to Phi Beta Kappa. He was then chosen to serve as law clerk to United States Supreme Court Justice Sherman Minton for one year and later returned to practice law in Chicago. He and his family live in Evanston, Illinois.

JONATHAN MIRSKY, Associate Professor of History and Chinese at Dartmouth College, is also Co-director of the College's East Asia Language and Area Studies Center. He teaches Chinese language, Chinese intellectual history and Southeast Asian history, and is currently engaged in research on American foreign policy in Southeast Asia. He co-authored *Peace in Vietnam*, published in 1966, and is a contributor to *America's Asia, Laos: War and Revolution,* and *Crimes of War,* all published in 1971. He has published articles in *The China Quarterly, Journal of the American Oriental Society, The New York Review of Books,* and *The Nation.* Professor Mirsky lived in Asia from 1958 to 1961, traveling in Indonesia, Thailand, Taiwan, Japan and Malaya. He returned to Asia in 1965, 1967, 1968 and 1969, visiting South Vietnam, Laos, Thailand, and Australia. Since 1968 he has three times held discussions with the Hanoi and National Liberation Front (NLF) delegations to the Paris peace talks. Before coming to Dartmouth in 1968, Professor Mirsky lectured at Taiwan Normal University, 1959–1960, and co-directed the Inter-University Chinese School in Taiwan, 1961–1962. In 1962 he was Tutor at Cambridge University, following which he taught for four years at the University of Pennsylvania's Graduate School of Oriental Studies.

*PARREN MITCHELL was elected from Baltimore, Maryland, to the United States House of Representatives in November of 1970. He serves on both the House Banking and Currency Committee and the Select Committee on Small Business. An opponent of the Vietnam war, Representative Mitchell in 1971 initiated a suit—in which he was joined by twelve other Congressmen—against the President and the Secretaries of Defense, State, Army and Navy, charging that by their continuance of the war without express legislative consent, they had unsurped that exclusive power of the Congress to declare war. The suit, dismissed by a United States District Judge, is presently being appealed. Representative Mitchell has served as the Executive Director of the Maryland Human Relations Commission, and as the first head of the Baltimore City Community Action Agency. Prior to his election to Congress, Congressman Mitchell was Professor of Sociology and Assistant Director of the Urban Studies Institute, Morgan State College. In Maryland, he currently serves on the boards of Americans for Democratic Action and the Committee for a Sane Nuclear Policy (SANE).

RT. REV. PAUL J. MOORE, JR. was elected Bishop Coadjutor of the Episcopalian Diocese of New York in December 1969. He was consecrated Bishop in 1964, having been elected Suffragan of the Diocese of Washington in September of 1963. Bishop Moore graduated from Yale University in 1941 with a B.A. He received an STB from General Theological Seminary in 1949 and an honorary D.D. in 1960. Virginia Theological Seminary honored him with a D.D. in 1964. He has served on numerous boards and committees, and as chairman of the Commission on the Delta Ministry, the National Council of Churches' ministry in Mississippi. He is presently a member of the Yale Corporation and a trustee of the General Theologi-

cal Seminary. During World War II he served in the United States Marine Corps from 1941 to 1945. In the summer of 1970 he was chairman of a Peace Mission to South Vietnam and presently serves on the National Committee of Clergy and Laymen Concerned.

MARCUS G. RASKIN is co-founder and presently co-director of the Institute for Policy Studies in Washington, D. C. He served as legislative counsel to twelve Democratic Congressmen from 1958 until 1961 and was staff editor of *The Liberal Papers* on foreign policy, published in 1961. A member of the National Security Council staff from 1961 to 1962, he served as education adviser in the Office of the President and was a member of the United States Disarmament Delegation in Geneva in 1962. In 1963 he was the education advisor to the Bureau of the Budget, Executive Office of the President, where he drafted comprehensive education legislation. From 1963–1965 he was a member of the Presidential Panel on Educational Research and Development and a consultant to the Office of Science and Technology on Education in the White House. He served on the board of directors and was a contributing editor of *Ramparts* Magazine from 1965 to 1968. He is the author of many books, including: *After Twenty Years: Alternatives to the Cold War in Europe* (with Richard Barnet), 1965; *The Viet-Nam Reader* (with Bernard Fall); *Being and Doing: From Deliberation to Liberation,* 1970; and most recently, *Washington Plans an Aggressive War* (with Richard Barnet, Ralph Stavins and other Institute people), 1971.

*BENJAMIN S. ROSENTHAL was elected as a Democrat-Liberal to the House of Representatives in the 87th Congress at a special election held in February of 1962. He is a Member of the House Foreign Affairs Committee, chairs its Subcommittee

on Europe, and also serves on the subcommittees on Inter-American Affairs and on International Organizations and Movements. He is also a member of the House Government Operations Committee, serving on its Subcommittees on Legislation and Military Operations, and Intergovernmental Relations. Mr. Rosenthal led many fights for improved consumer protection laws as chairman of a Special Inquiry on Consumer Representation in the Federal Government. He is currently the chairman of the Democratic Study Group's Consumer Task Force. An early opponent of the Vietnam war, Mr. Rosenthal is also a member of the steering committee of Members of Congress for Peace through Law. He is a participant in Anglo-American Parliamentary Conferences and a leader in efforts to bring European Community parliamentarians together regularly with United States Congressmen. Prior to his election to Congress from Queens, New York, he was an attorney in New York.

WILLIAM FITTS RYAN, re-elected to his sixth term in November, 1970, with an 80 percent majority, is a member of the House Judiciary Committee and the House Committee on Interior and Insular Affairs. He serves on the executive committee of the Democratic Study Group in the House of Representatives. In 1960 he became the first reform Democrat elected to Congress, and was the reform Democratic candidate for mayor in 1965. One of the earliest and most vocal opponents in the House against the Vietnam war, Ryan was the first public official to urge Senator Robert F. Kennedy to challenge President Johnson in the 1968 primaries. Elected as a delegate to the Chicago convention, he helped lead the campaign to nominate Senator Eugene McCarthy and spoke for the minority plank on Vietnam. Besides sponsoring and co-sponsoring over the years measures designed to bring about

[195]

an end to the Vietnam war, Congressman Ryan was the first House Member to introduce a bill to provide for a guaranteed annual income.

ANTHONY J. RUSSO, JR. is a 1964 graduate of the Woodrow Wilson School of Public and International Affairs in the graduate school at Princeton University. He was on the research staff of the Rand Corporation between June 1964 and January 1969, spending twenty-four months of that period in South Vietnam where he conducted studies of Viet Cong motivation and morale, the relationship between popular support for the Viet Cong and socioeconomic factors, and the effectiveness of the United States crop spray program. He then became the head of the probation operations research section of the Los Angeles County Probation Department. In 1971 he was sentenced to jail on a contempt citation by Judge William P. Gray of Los Angeles for refusing to testify before a grand jury against Daniel Ellsberg. On Oct. 1, 1971, he was released from Terminal Island Federal Prison in San Pedro, California, after agreeing to testify before the grand jury under certain conditions. He has taken public responsibility, along with Dr. Ellsberg, for making the Pentagon Papers available to the American people.

*JOHN F. SEIBERLING was first elected to Congress on November 3, 1970, from Akron, Ohio. Never before a candidate for public office, Congressman Seiberling defeated twenty-year incumbent Representative William Ayres. He serves on both the House Judiciary Committee and the House Science and Astronautics Committee. Prior to his election, he had been active in the Democratic Party in Ohio, working in several congressional and mayoral campaigns during the 1960's. He was a member of the Goodyear Tire and Rubber Company's

legal staff for sixteen years, specializing in anti-trust law. He formerly practiced law in New York City, where he also worked as an attorney with the Legal Aid Society. A veteran of World War II who rose from the rank of private to major, he helped organize the Normandy Invasion and won the Legion of Merit, Bronze Star and three battle stars. The governments of France and Belgium also decorated him for outstanding service. He received his law degree from Columbia University in 1947.

GENERAL NGUYEN CHANH THI is a native of Hue. He was imprisoned by the Communists in 1945, supported Diem and then led an abortive coup against him in 1960, fleeing to Cambodia where he was imprisoned. After the Diem assassination in 1963, he was called back to Vietnam from this first exile by Big Minh. Considered one of the most important generals in Saigon from 1964–1966, he was present at the meeting called by Ambassador Maxwell Taylor in 1964 and since made famous by the publication of the Pentagon Papers. One of Thi's assets was that he was extremely popular among the Buddhists of Central Vietnam. He survived the Khanh coup and subsequently spent his days in Vietnam as commander of the I Corps. After a showdown with his rival, Nguyen Cao Ky, General Thi was exiled in 1966. While presently residing in Washington, D.C., General Thi plans to return to Saigon sometime in the near future.

TRUONG DINH HUNG DAVID was born in Can-Tho, northern Vietnam, on September 2, 1945, the Independence Day of Vietnam. He studied at schools in both Saigon and Paris. In 1965 he enrolled at Stanford University in California and received his B.A. in economics in June of 1968. Since 1969 he has set up The Vietnam Political Freedom Committee which

works in the United States for the release of South Vietnam's political prisoners. Mr. Truong is also a lecturer and free-lance writer. His father, Truong Dinh Dzu, 1967 presidential runner-up in the South Vietnam elections, who had advocated the bombing halt in North Vietnam, direct negotiations with the National Liberation Front and a coalition government has been imprisoned since 1967.

APPENDIX ONE

Congress' Interest
in *The New York Times* and
The Washington Post Cases

CONGRESS' INTEREST IN THE NEW YORK TIMES AND THE
WASHINGTON POST CASES

Mr. ECKHARDT. Mr. Speaker, on Saturday, June 26, the Supreme
Court heard the New York Times and the Washington Post cases
concerning the publication of the secret Pentagon report on the
Vietnam war. Just as we did in the District Court for the Southern
District of New York, the District Court for the District of Colum-
bia, the District Court for the District of Massachusetts, the Court of
Appeals for the Second Circuit, and the Court of Appeals for the
District of Columbia, I and 26 other Members filed a brief as amici
curiae on the side of the Times and the Post.

As the brief indicates, we believe that Members of Congress have
a very special and unique interest in having these documents and "a
particular and profound interest in having their constituents obtain
all the information necessary to perform their functions as voters
and citizens." I urge all of my colleagues to read this brief so as to
better understand our sincere concern:
[In the Supreme Court of the United States, October Term, 1970,
No. 1873]

Rep. Bob Eckhardt, *Congressional Record*, June 28, 1971, pp. E. 6703–6706.

The New York Times Co., et al., Petitioner, v. United States of America, Respondent.

United States of America, Petitioner, v. The Washington Post Company, et al, Respondent.

BRIEF OF 27 MEMBERS OF CONGRESS AS AMICI CURIAE

This brief is filed on behalf of the following Members of Congress: Phillip Burton, John Dow, Bob Eckhardt, Don Edwards, Michael Harrington, Robert Kastenmeier, Edward Koch, Abner Mikva, Benjamin Rosenthal, William F. Ryan, James Abourezk, Bella S. Abzug, William R. Anderson, Herman Badillo, Jonathan B. Bingham, William Clay, Ronald V. Dellums, Sam Gibbons, Ella T. Grasso, Seymour Halpern, Peter Kyros, Parren Mitchell, Bertram L. Podell, Charles B. Rangel, Donald W. Riegle, Jr., James H. Scheuer, and Lester L. Wolff.

INTEREST OF AMICI

The Members of Congress, on whose behalf this brief is filed, have a vital interest in the outcome of these cases, distinct from that of the plaintiff, the defendants, or the general public. As members of the national legislature they must have information of the kind involved in these suits in order to carry out their law-making and other functions in the legislative branch of the government. They seek to vindicate here a legislative right to know.

In addition as elected representatives of the people in their districts, Members of Congress have a particular and profound interest in having their constituents obtain all the information necessary to perform their functions as voters and citizens. More than any other officials of government, Members of Congress have relations with the public that gives them a crucial concern with the public's right to know.

We agree with the position of the defendants New York Times and Washington Post that the courts have no inherent authority, absent a statute, to prevent publication of the documents involved here, and that no such statutory authority exists. We confine our argument, however to the broader constitutional issues and urge

upon the Court three fundamental propositions: (1) that information which comes to light other than by strictly lawful process is nevertheless entitled to the full protection of the First Amendment; (2) that the attempt by the Government to suppress publication of these documents violates both the legislative and the public right to know; and (3) that the doctrine of prior restraint forbids advance censorship of material published by the press.

I. INFORMATION WHICH COMES TO LIGHT OTHER THAN BY STRICTLY LEGAL PROCESS IS NEVERTHELESS ENTITLED TO THE FULL PROTECTION OF THE FIRST AMENDMENT

The general approach which ought to govern solution of the problem now before the Court has been well expressed by James Madison in his Report on the Virginia Resolutions:

"In every State, probably, in the Union, the press has exerted a freedom in canvassing the merits and measures of public men of every description which has not been confined to the strict limits of the common law. On this footing the freedom of the press has stood; on this footing it yet stands. . . . Some degree of abuse is inseparable from the proper use of everything, and in no instance is this more true than in that of the press. It has accordingly been decided by the practice of the States, that it is better to leave a few of its noxious branches to their luxuriant growth than, by pruning them away, to injure the vigour of those yielding the proper fruits." [1]

The Government's approach has been quite different. The Government conceives of the problem as if the only issue were one of stolen goods. It bases its claim upon a proprietary interest in the information involved, urges that it is entitled to recover its stolen property, and contends that neither Members of Congress nor the general public can have any right to the purloined information. [2]

The Government's position might be valid if all that was involved were a stolen automobile. It might even be sound as applied to the

---

[1] Report on the Virginia Resolutions, Madison's Works, vol. iv, 544.

[2] After commencement of the proceedings the President, as a matter of grace, made the materials available to members of Congress. *N.Y. Times*, June 24, 1971.

physical documents themselves, or to a copyrighted manuscript of a private author. But this approach has no valid application to *information* about public events. Such information, whether or not it comes to light within "the strict limits of the common law," is part of the common fund of knowledge available to the general public in its role as ultimate decision-maker. This information, therefore, comes within the ambit of the First Amendment and the issue moves to a higher, constitutional level.

It is well known to observers of public affairs that vast amounts of information become available to Congress and the public in a manner which does not conform to the Executive's national security classification scheme. The affidavits of Max Frankel, Benjamin Bradlee, and other newsmen on file in the present proceedings make this entirely clear. Indeed, one of the principal functions of a free press in this country is to ferret out information which the Executive wishes to conceal. Executive officials themselves consistently disclose classified information, or engineer leaks, for the purpose of influencing public decision-making. Much other classified material emerges in memoirs, government documents taken when the official leaves office, and similar sources. The existence of such a communications system in fact marks the difference between a free press and a controlled press, between a democratic system of free expression and a totalitarian system of controlled expression.

The Executive regulations on classification can govern the internal operation of the Executive agencies. They cannot, under the First Amendment, control communication of information outside the government. To put it colloquially, a cat in the bag cannot be treated the same way as a cat outside the bag. Once the information gets outside the Executive—once the Executive loses its control for any reason—the information becomes part of the public domain. [3]

The results that flow from this state of affairs are twofold. First,

---

[3] We are not discussing here the right of Congress, one of its members, or the general public to force the Executive to disclose information under powers inherent in the legislature, the First Amendment, or statutes such as the Freedom of Information Act.

once having lost control of the information the Government can, as a practical matter, rarely get the information back. The events of the past few weeks fully demonstrate the truth of this proposition. Second, whatever the rights of the Executive may be with respect to the person who first obtained the information in breach of the classification rules, the Executive should not be allowed to try to regain control of the information through muzzling the press. Such an effort, involving suppression of information at whatever point it crops up in the communications system, under the guise of fact or opinion or even art or literature, could only be accomplished by the kind of controls that are characteristic of a police state.

II. THE ATTEMPT BY THE EXECUTIVE TO SUPPRESS PUBLICATION OF THESE DOCUMENTS VIOLATES BOTH THE LEGISLATIVE AND THE PUBLIC RIGHT TO KNOW

The defendants in these proceedings have, quite naturally, stressed the protection which the First Amendment extends to the speaker, the writer and the publisher of information. This case also presents, in a way no other case in our history has before, the other side of the First Amendment coin,—the right to listen, to hear, and to obtain information. Two aspects of this right to know are involved here. We discuss first the right of Members of Congress and second the right of the general public.

A. The legislative right to know

The legislative right to know derives from the position and function of the legislative branch in the general structure of our government. It has been recognized many times in the decisions of this Court. See, e.g., *Watkins v. United States*, 354 U.S. 178 (1957). The legislative right to know also derives from the First Amendment. That constitutional mandate was designed to maintain an effective system of freedom of expression and members of the legislature are entitled, as are private citizens, to share its benefits and protections.

It would be hard to overestimate the importance to our form of government of the legislative right to know. That right is indispensable to the performance of every function of the legislative branch.

Clearly legislative access to information ought to be at least on a par with that of the Executive. For the legislative function is not only to initiate the basic policies which the Executive branch must follow, but to review the administration of those policies by the Executive and revise them in the light of that knowledge.

The legislative right to know is of particular importance at this period of development in our national affairs. The constant growth of the executive power has been a major characteristic of our age. More and more the people of our country have been concerned that the expansion of executive power has upset the original balance contemplated by the framers of our Constitution that monopoly of power in the Executive has resulted in the government losing touch with the needs and desires of its own citizens, and that enhanced power in our elected representatives is imperative to restore a healthy division of authority in government.

There are a number of reasons for this unparalleled and dangerous growth of Executive power in the United States. There can be no doubt, however, that one of the principal reasons is the far greater access of the Executive to information, and its unwillingness to share that knowledge with Congress and the public. In today's world, control of the information process is the key to power.

It is crucial to note, also, that the legislature cannot adequately perform its function upon the basis of "official" information submitted to it by the Executive branch. Every observer of government knows that "official" information, in most situations, tells only half the story. And bureaucracy, by the nature of the institution, tends to reveal only what it believes will support its own position and advance its own policies. A realistic fund of information must depend upon materials which lie far below the surface. The system of checks and balances cannot rest upon such bland sources of information as Executive hand-outs.

In this process of obtaining fuller, richer and more realistic information the press plays a vital role. It is not too much to say that this is perhaps the most important function of a free press. Obviously it is not a function that can be performed by a press under governmental constraint.

There is no need to stress here that the documents involved in these proceedings could not be more relevant to the issues now pending in Congress. Termination of the war in Vietnam, extension of Selective Service, appropriations for the conduct of the war, and numerous other questions are before the House and the Senate at this very moment. In addition, broader problems going to the respective powers of Congress and the President in connection with the making of war and the conduct of foreign relations are pressing for attention. It thwarts common sense that the information here in question should be withheld from Members of Congress.

In sum, to close off access to the kind of material the Government is now attempting to suppress would cripple the legislature in the performance of its constitutional functions. It would go far to relegate the legislative branch to second rate status in relation to the Executive, to jeopardize the balance of power between the branches of governments and to alter the whole constitutional structure.

B. The public right to know

The public right to know has been repeatedly recognized by this Court as a vital aspect of our system of freedom of expression. As Mr. Justice Brennan said in his concurring opinion in *Lamont v. Postmaster General:*

"It is true that the First Amendment contains no specific guarantee of access to publications. However, the protection of the Bill of Rights goes beyond the specific guarantees to protect from congressional abridgment those equally fundamental personal rights necessary to make the express guarantees fully meaningful. . . . I think the right to receive publications is such a fundamental right. The dissemination of ideas can accomplish nothing if otherwise willing addressees are not free to receive and consider them. It would be a barren marketplace of ideas that had only sellers and no buyers." 381 U.S. 301, 308 (1965).

The public right to know was the basis of the decision upholding the fairness doctrine in *Red Lion Broadcasting Co. v. F.C.C.,* 395 U.S. 367 (1969), and the right to read what one pleases in *Stanley v. Georgia,* 394 U.S. 557 (1969). Lower Federal courts have like-

[205]

wise applied the principle to uphold the interests of the public as recipients of information in an untrammeled system of freedom of expression. See, e.g., *Office of Communications of United Church of Christ v. F.C.C.*, 359 F. 2d 994 (D.C. Cir. 1966); *Mandel v. Mitchell*, 39 L.W. 2530 (1971).

Members of Congress, of course, have the same interests as other citizens in protection of the right to know. They also have a particular interest as members of the legislative branch. Effective performance of their duties as elected representatives depends upon a knowledgeable constituency. Members of Congress and the people they represent must operate on a shared basis of understanding, upon a common wavelength. It is vital to the functioning of a democratic system that the electors have enough information to grasp the issues upon which their representatives are voting. It is likewise essential to the Member of Congress that he relate to the ideas and responses of his constituents. This reciprocal relation depends upon the fullest access possible to a common store of information. The public right to know, therefore, takes on a special importance when it concerns matters pending before the legislature.

Once again, it is difficult to imagine any information more relevant to the public right to know than the documents which the Government is here trying to keep the public from seeing.

The precise degree of protection afforded by the doctrine of the right to know, as embodied in the first Amendment, has not yet been fully developed. It may be some years before the specific rules can be worked out. Yet the starting point is clear. It is that members of the public have, as a general proposition, the right to know all information upon which decisions that affect their lives and property are based. This is the fundamental premise of a democratic system. Exceptions to the general rule must be narrow and specific. They would be recognized only in such special areas as military weapons and operations, current negotiations with a foreign country, or damage to individual reputation by premature disclosure of investigative data.

Wherever the line of exceptions may be drawn it has not been reached in these cases. Judge Gurfein and Judge Gesell have both

found, after a full hearing, that no substantial breach of national security is involved. The withholding of the information here in question has a maximum impact upon the constitutional right to know and the function it is designed to perform. There is no sound ground for not giving full effect to the constitutional principle in these cases.

A genuine and whole hearted insistence upon maintaining the right to know is vital to the welfare of the nation and its ability to cope with the many problems that now confront it. Much of the frustration, mistrust and misunderstanding that prevails in many quarters of the land today is due to our failure to keep the decision-making process on a more open and observable basis. Vigorous enforcement of the constitutional right to know would go far to restore confidence in our institutions and evoke support from the people who are most affected by their operation.

III. THE DOCTRINE OF PRIOR RESTRAINT FORBIDS ADVANCE CENSORSHIP
OF THE MATERIAL HERE INVOLVED

The doctrine of prior restraint, growing out of revulsion to the English censorship laws, holds that governmental restrictions cannot be imposed upon expression in advance of publication. Even though the expression may be subject to subsequent punishment or can otherwise be restricted at a later point, it cannot be proscribed prior to publication. The doctrine was made part of our constitutional law in *Near v. Minnesota*, 283 U.S. 697 (1931). It has since been repeatedly confirmed. See e.g., *Lovell v. Griffin*, 303 U.S. 444 (1938); *Kunz v. N.Y.*, 340 U.S 290 (1951); *Carroll v. President and Commissioners of Princess Anne*, 393 U.S. 175 (1968).

The theory of the prior restraint doctrine is that a system which requires a publisher to submit his material in advance to a government censor is so repressive by its very nature as to be inevitably destructive of free expression. The reasons for this have been stated as follows:

"A system of prior restraint is in many ways more inhibiting than a system of subsequent punishment: It is likely to bring under government scrutiny a far wider range of expression; it shuts off communication before it takes place; suppression by a stroke of the pen

is more likely to be applied than suppression through a criminal process; the system allows less opportunity for public appraisal and criticism; the dynamics of the system drive toward excesses, as the history of all censorship shows." [4]

So oppressive is a scheme of prior restraint that it is not an exaggeration to say that it smacks of totalitarian rather than democratic methods of control.

All the parties to these cases, and all the courts that have passed on the various aspects of them, recognize the critical importance of the doctrine of prior restraint. The issue here has turned, not on the validity of the doctrine, but upon whether an exception should be made to it in the case of national security. In a dictum in *Near v. Minnesota* the Court stated that there might be exceptional cases where the doctrine would not be applied, mentioning "actual obstruction to [the] recruiting service or the publication of the sailing dates of transports or the number and location of troops;" "obscene publications;" and "incitements to acts of violence and the overthrow by force of orderly government." 283 U.S. at 716. An actual exception has been made in the case of motion picture censorship boards to the extent of upholding laws which require advance screening of films against possible illegal obscenity. *Times Film Corp. v. City of Chicago*, 365 U.S. 43 (1961); *Freeman v. Maryland*, 380 U.S. 51 (1965). No other exceptions have been permitted. It has never been suggested by any court that the press could be subject to any form of advance censorship.

In the cases at bar, for the first time in the history of this country, various formulations have been proposed for an exception applying broadly to national security matters. The Government, if we understand its position correctly, urges that an exception be made for any classified document would per se constitute such a breach. Judge Gurfein would allow an exception for "information or documents absolutely vital to current national security." The Court of Appeals for the Second Circuit approved censorship of items which

---

[4] T. I. Emerson, *The System of Freedom of Expression* (1970), p. 506.

"pose such grave and immediate danger to the security of the United States as to warrant their publication being enjoined."

We submit that any of the above formulations would effectively nullify the prior restraint doctrine in the area of national security matters and would gravely jeopardize the whole system of freedom of expression. The Government's proposal would permit an injunction against the publication of any classified material unless the publisher could show that the classification was arbitrary and capricious. If this Court sanctions such a rule the press will be at the mercy of the Department of Justice. The Government will be in a position to leak any classified information that serves its own purposes and shut off countervailing information. The Executive would be arrogating to itself dictatorial power over the dissemination of large quantities of information bearing upon national defense, foreign policy, and most of the other important issues of the day.

The formulations of Judge Gurfein and the Court of Appeals for the Second Circuit, although more stringent on their face, would be almost equally destructive of a free press in America. We do not make this statement lightly. We ask the Court to consider carefully how the doctrines put forward in these courts below would operate in practice. Under any of these formulations the Executive can hold up publication simply by alleging that a serious breach of national security would occur. The Court would then issue a restraining order, allow the Government to present its case, and then decide whether there was sufficient danger to warrant issuance of an injunction against publication. *This process in itself is a system of prior restraint.* It involves an examination of the material by Executive officials, an order to withhold publication, and a governmental decision as to whether the material could be published or not. The exception has swallowed up the rule.

Moreover, most of the proceeding—certainly the critical parts—would take place in camera. Both the New York Times and the Washington Post cases followed this procedure, on the ground that otherwise the injury to national security would occur in the course of hearing the case. Only the defendants and their counsel

were permitted to attend the in camera session. More than that, no one was allowed to be present unless he was first given security clearance by the Government. Hence the plaintiff in the case was able to dictate what individual defendants, and what counsel, were entitled to participate in determination of the issue. Such a procedure can hardly be recommended in a democratic society.

In any event, we submit that any rule for allowing exceptions which would create a system of prior restraint in the very process of applying the rule cannot be reconciled with the First Amendment. We do not say that under no circumstances can an exception to the prior restraint doctrine be justified. But it seems clear that a rule based, as are the rules suggested above, upon the gravity of the breach of security can only operate to install a full, not exceptional, system of prior restraint in the whole "national security" area.

The task of formulating a workable rule for exceptions is a complex one. Any such rule would probably have to be couched in terms of allowing the exception only for certain very specific kinds of information. As the Court suggested in *Near*, information on troop movements in times of war might fall within the excepted category. Perhaps details concerning the design of military weapons would be another category. Beyond the immediate area of military operations there should be few, if any, classes of information subject to advance restraint. Very little consideration has been given to the problem and no one is in a position to give a satisfactory answer at this time.

Even Judge Gesell's formulation in his opinion refusing a preliminary injunction would raise troubling questions unless considered in the context of his rulings taken as a whole. Judge Gesell, after considering these matters in the preliminary injunction stages, gave a stricter formulation than did Judge Gurfein, requiring a "showing of an immediate, grave threat to the national security . . . in close and narrowly defined circumstances." Applying this test Judge Gesell correctly refused to apply any restraint.

The Government's complaint contained no allegation of any concrete facts which would suggest a breach of national security in any

specific area that might conceivably be subject to an exception to the prior restraint rule. Under such circumstances no temporary restraining order should have been issued and the complaint should have been dismissed. Therefore, the decision of the Court of Appeals for the District of Columbia should be further elucidated. "Closely and narrowly defined circumstances" must be shown to be as narrow as those exceptional circumstances alluded to in *Near v. Minnesota.*

We urge the Court to follow this course. Especially we urge the Court not to accept any formulation of exceptions to the prior restraint rule which will undermine the force and vitality of that traditional doctrine.

CONCLUSION

The issues involved in these cases go to the heart of the decision-making process in this country. The tendency of government in recent years had been toward ever more secrecy in its operations, and toward a consequent monopoly of power in the hands of a few high Executive officials. We suggest that this direction of events is fraught with danger. Secrecy in government is fundamentally anti-democratic. It perpetuates bureaucratic errors and leads ultimately to disaster. It is time our constitutional doctrines were called ino play in opposition to those forces and invoked to promote conditions under which an open, representative and balanced government will be assured.

We respectfully submit that the complaints in these proceedings should be dismissed.

BOB ECKHARDT
Washington, D.C.
THOMAS I. EMERSON.
New Haven, Conn.

Attorneys for Amici.
June 25, 1971.

A Right to Know as Well as
A Right to Publish—
The Washington Post Case

A RIGHT TO KNOW AS WELL AS A RIGHT TO PUBLISH—THE WASHINGTON POST CASE

Mr. ECKHARDT. Mr. Speaker, as you know, 27 Members of Congress filed a motion of intervention on June 21 in the case of United States of America against the Washington Post, et al. in the U.S. District Court for the District of Columbia.

This case has particular interest to all Members of the House of Representatives and I urge that they read the motion for intervention and the accompanying brief to be printed at this point in the RECORD:

[U.S. District Court for the District of
Columbia Civil Action No. 1235–71]

BRIEF IN SUPPORT OF MOTION FOR INTERVENTION

United States of America, Plaintiff against the Washington Post, et al., Defendants.

STATEMENT OF THE CASE

This is a motion for intervention by 27 Members of Congress. It

---

Rep. Bob Eckhardt, *Congressional Record,* June 23, 1971, pp. E6356–6360.

is movants' contention that their position is distinct and different from that of The Washington Post and they are entitled, as a matter of right, to intervene. The Washington Post's interest in freedom of speech and of the press here is the interest of the *speaker* or the publisher not to be restricted by governmental action abridging freedom of speech. The interest of the Members of Congress seeking to intervene is the other side of the coin: the interest in not being deprived of information which would normally flow to them but for an intervening act of government restraining that flow.

The difference in position of movants adds the dimension of urgency, and this is the important reason why Members of Congress, speaking from the platform of particular factual injury, are entitled to participate in this case.

To capsulate the point, a brief analysis of the situation must be set forth:

Two important courses of events transpired contemporaneously, events of the stuff which affects the fate of the nation. The first was dramatic and fast-moving: the revelation of the existence of the Defense Department's Task Force Study on Vietnam ordered by Secretary McNamara which gives piercing insight into the gut workings of war making and the conduct of foreign affairs by the President, the rest of his civilian executive establishment, and the Joint Chiefs of Staff. The second important course of events was, and is, the continuing deliberate process of decision-making in a democracy. As Judge Wright said in his dissent:

"At a time when the American people and their Congress are in the midst of a pitched debate over the war, the history of the war, however disillusioning, is crucial. The executive department, which brought us into the war and which would be primarily "embarrassed" by publication of the material in question, must not be allowed to bury that history at such a time. Democracy works only when the people are informed."

It is the primary purpose of this brief to show that the interest of movants, a pressing public need for immediate access to matters directly and importantly affecting ongoing process in Congress, is different from that of the defendant, The Washington Post; and that

[213]

"injury in fact" results to these movants by *any* delay of the flow of information free of an unconstitutional prior restraint.

It may be possible to argue that The Washington Post and The New York Times are not substantially injured if the courts ultimately determine that a prior restraint on the publication of the articles concerning this Task Force Study is unconstitutional. Not so with these movants: Their deliberations and actions in participating in the formulation of national policy are crippled and inhibited by not having highly pertinent information which is *known* to exist. Such is not only directly injurious to each of them as a Congressman representing a constituency but also tends to undermine the entire representative process. The right of the people to secure information necessary to the effective exercise of their function as citizens in a democracy is interrelated with the right of their representative to act on information normally available to himself *and* to those whom he represents.

ARGUMENT

In order for any party to proceed in a case before a court there must be (1) a case or controversy, [1] and (2) a complaining party who either presents a case in which his standing is quite clear or who proffers for judicial determination a question concerning his own legal status.

I. THIS MATTER CLEARLY INVOLVES A CASE OR CONTROVERSY.

There is, of course, no question but that the case before this Court falls within the constitutional grant of jurisdiction to federal courts of certain "cases, in law and and equity" and "certain controversies." The United States has contended that The Washington Post is wrongfully in possession of certain governmental documents and should be enjoined from publishing them. As a result the Court

---

[1] There must be one qualification. In the case of an intervenor it has been held that there may be sufficient interest to justify intervention even if there would not be a case or controversy between the plaintiff and the intervenors as principal parties so long as the case between the original parties itself presents a case or controversy. *Ford Motor Co.* v. *Bisanz Bros.*, 249 F. 2d 22 (8th Cir. 1957); Shapiro, "Some Thoughts on Intervention Before Courts, Agencies, and Arbitrators," 81 Har. L. Rev. 721 (1968), at p. 726, and the authorities cited therein.

of Appeals for the District of Columbia has granted a temporary re-straining order. The Washington Post asserts that it is entitled to publish the materials as a part of its exercise of freedom of speech and freedom of the press. There being, therefore, a case of contro-versy before this Court, the only question respecting these movants' intervention is the question of their standing and their right to inter-vene.

II. INTERVENORS [2] HAVE A DISTINCT AND SEPARATE JUSTICIABLE INTEREST

As we have said, the defendant's interest in its First Amendment right is to speak or to publish free of a prior restraint abridging its right of freedom of speech. Intervenors' interest is the other side of the coin: the interest is not being deprived of information which would normally flow to them but for an intervening act of govern-ment restraining that flow. It is our contention that this right is as carefully protected by the First Amendment as is the publisher's right. The Court in *Stanley* v. *Georgia*, 394 U.S. 557, 564 (1969) said: "It is now well established that the Constitution protects the right to receive information and ideas. [3]

That interest is not, at present, represented in this litigation and as we shall show it is a distinct and different interest than that of The Washington Post. The proposed intervenors would represent that fundamental interest, the public's right to know. But they would also represent an even more critical interest. As elected representatives of the people, charged with responsibility for voting on matters now pending in the Congress which will vitally affect the lives of their constituents, [4] they must have the information which

---

[2] Since the status of intervenors argued for here is the basis for the considerations and arguments that these movants would make in the case, it is more meaningful and natural to refer to them, somewhat prematurely, as "intervenors"; and we shall, with deference, so designate them in this brief.

[3] See, to the same effect, *Lamont* v. *Postmaster General*, 381 U.S. 301 (1965). *United States* v. *Dellapia*, 433 F. 2d 1252, 1258, n. 25 (2d Cir. 1970); *Caldwell* v. *United States*, 434 F. 2d 1081, 1089 (9th Cir. 1970). *Hiett* v. *United States*, 415 F. 2d 664, 671 (5th Cir. 1968).

[4] E.g., the bills described in the affidavit of Congressman BOB ECKHARDT, submitted herewith.

the plaintiff has asked this Court to suppress, so that they can make informed, intelligent decisions.

To deny them that information would be destructive of the public interest, because it would require them to continue to make groping policy decisions with respect to the Indochina war in a twilight area not fully illuminated by candid executive disclosure. In crucial areas of policy making Congress would have to continue to act in partial ignorance of the historic context in which they are acting. [5]

It is now clear that such a deprivation of flow of information which would exist but for governmental restraint constitutes a justiciable interest. *Mandel* v. *Mitchell,* decided by a three-judge court in the Eastern District of New York, [6] is directly in point. There certain university professors complained of the refusal to permit an alien, Mandel, to come into the country and express certain economic, international, and governmental doctrines of world communism. Mandel was denied a non-immigrant visitor's visa under the asserted authority of Section 212(a) (28) of the Immigration and Nationality Act. The professors alleged that they and other citizens desired to have Mandel speak at universities and other forums to hear his views and to engage in free and open academic exchange and they charged that the section of the Act excluding from admission to the United States aliens who are, or at any time were, members of described classes of aliens identified with certain leftist and extremist political doctrines is invalid under the 1st and 5th Amendments and that it imposes a prior restraint on constitutionally protected communication.

In response to defendant's attack on the professors' "standing to sue" the Court said:

---

[5] For cases noting the special interest of public representatives and agencies as intervenors, see *Cascade Nat. Gas* v. *El Paso Nat. Gas,* 386 U.S. 129 (1967); *Securities and Exchange Commission* v. *United States Realty & Imp. Co.,* 310 U.S. 434 (1940); and *Nuesse* v. *Camp,* 128 U.S. App. D.C. 172, 385 F. 2d 694 (D.C. Cir. 1967).

[6] _____ F Supp. _____ (E.D.N.Y., 1971), 39 LW 2531, et seq.

"Since the First Amendment is not in its primary and most significant aspect a grant by the Constitution to the citizens of individual rights of self-expression but on the contrary reflects that total retention by the people as sovereign to themselves of the right to free and open debate of political questions, the issue of "standing to sue" is immediately seen to be unreal. The concern of the First Amendment is not with a nonresident alien's individual and personal interest in entering and being heard, but with the rights of the citizens of the country to have the alien enter and to hear him explain and seek to defend his views. * * *

"Mandel's status as a party does not rest on any individual right to enter (for he has none) but exists only as against the efforts to exclude him on a ground that denies to citizens of this country their primary rights to hear Mandel and debate with him. Here the plaintiffs other than Mandel are directly involved with Mandel's entry because they have invited him, and they expect to participate in meetings with him or expect to be among his auditors. No more is required to establish their standing. Cf. Snyder v. Board of Trustees, 286 F. Supp. at 931–932 (N.D. Ill. 1968); Smith v. University of Tennessee, 300 F. Supp. 777 (E.D. Tenn. 1969)"

But the fact that Congressmen are themselves deprived of information is not the sole injury that these movants suffer. As we have said, the granting of an injunction would cause injury in fact to these intervenors in limiting their resources and their tools for solving problems relegated to them under the Constitution. [7]

But, in addition, it would injure them in this respect: Event if it were possible for Members of Congress to obtain similar information through private and confidential sources these intervenors would have to act on this information without their constituents knowing the

---

[7] Section 8 of Article I of the Constitution places upon intervenors, together with other Members of Congress, duties requiring access to a wide range of information concerning, among other matters, the declaration of war, the raising and support of armies, the regulation of the land and naval forces, and the providing for, organizing, arming, governing and disciplining the militia.

[217]

same basic facts. The central tenet of democracy is that governments "derive their just powers from the consent of the governed," and of course Congress must repeatedly obtain this consent from the electorate. To staunch the flow of public information for any considerable time is to greatly impede the democratic process, because concerning great issues there is a considerable incubation time for the public to come to an understanding of the issues and to formulate opinion.

Public representatives properly intervene to protect their own function.

In *Cascade Nat. Gas* v. *El Paso Nat. Gas*, 386 U.S. 129 (1967), the Supreme Court noted that the 1966 amendments to Rule 24 were intended to liberalize intervention, and permitted the State of California to intervene, as of right, in an antitrust case as a representative of "the public interest in a competitive system." (386 U.S. at 135). Certainly the proposed intervenors are equally or more representative of the "public interest" in a democratic system, and thus entitled to intervene as of right.

In *Securities and Exchange Commission* v. *United States Realty & Imp. Co.*, 310 U.S. 434 (1940), decided many years before the liberalizing amendments to Rule 24, the District Court permitted the Securities and Exchange Commission to intervene in an "arrangement proceeding" under Chapter XI of the Bankruptcy Act. The Second Circuit reversed. The Supreme Court, agreeing with the District Court that intervention served the "public interest," reversed the Circuit Court. The Commission had intervened for two reasons: "to protect the interest of the public," and "to forestall the impairment of its own functions" under the Bankruptcy Act (310 U.S. at 445). [8] The Supreme Court, noting that the Commission was "charged with the performance of important public duties" (310 U.S. at 458), ruled that it was entitled to intervene in order "to

---

[8] Had the proceeding been filed under Chapter X, as the Commission contended it should have been, the Commission would have had a statutory right to oversee the proceeding.

object to an improper exercise of the court's jurisdiction which, if permitted to continue, . . . would defeat the public interests which the Commission was designated to represent" (310 U.S. at 459). The Supreme Court stressed that "the performance of its public duties" was a "sufficient interest" to justify the Commission's intervention even under the old, and restrictive, Rule 24.

The proposed intervenors herein assert the same grounds for intervention: to protect the "public interest" and to forestall "impairment" of their own functions. The "public duties" required of Congressmen by Article I, Section 8 of the United States Constitution are so much more vital to the public interest than the statutory duties entrusted to the SEC, that it would be inconceivable to exclude them from participation in this case.

Any doubts on that point are settled by *Nuesse* v. *Camp*, 128 U.S. App. D.C. 172, 385 F. 2d 694 (D.C. Cir. 1967). There a state-chartered bank sued to enjoin the United States Comptroller of the Currency from permitting a nationally chartered bank to open branch offices in that state. The State Commissioner of Banks moved to intervene. The District Court denied intervention and the Circuit Court reversed. The starting point there, as it should be here, was the Circuit Court's recognition that the purpose of the 1966 amendments to Rule 24 was to facilitate "full ventilation" of the legal and factual issues relevant to the issues before the court "by involving as many apparently concerned persons as is compatible with efficiency and due process," 128 U.S. App. D.C. 182, 178, 385 F. 2d at 704, 700.

To put it mildly, the Members of Congress who are the proposed intervenors in this case are, of course, "apparently concerned," and their express willingness to limit their participation insures the efficient resolution of these proceedings.

The Court of Appeals in *Nuesse* stated that "those opposing intervention" bore the "burden" of showing that the interests of the proposed intervenors are adequately represented by existing parties (128 U.S. App. D.C. at 180, 385 F. 2d at 702). Furthermore, the fact that the proposed intervenor wished to assert the "public inter-

ests," was, of itself, sufficient to differentiate his interest from that of the private litigants (128 U.S. App. D.C. at 181, 385 F. 2d at 703). Thus, even though there was a "tactical similarity" between the private interests of the state bank and the public interests of the state Commissioner of Banks, that tactical uniformity of interest would "not assure adequacy of representation" of the public interest by the private litigant (ibid.). Intervention was thus a matter of right, and, in addition, the Court ruled that denial of intervention was an abuse of discretion. In so ruling, the Court of Appeals set down an "appropriate standard," and a "more hospitable approach," guaranteeing intervention whenever a governmental representative seeks to protect the "public interest" (128 U.S. App. D.C. at 182–184, 383 F. 2d at 704–760). The "significant fact" which justified that approach was that the proposed intervenor was "a government official" who sought to "promote a relevant public interest" (128 U.S. App. D.C. at 183, 385 F. 2d at 705). Unless intervention would unduly expand or delay the proceedings, which would not be true here, intervention "is available when sought because an aspect of the public interest with which [the intervenor] is officially concerned is invoked in the litigation" (128 U.S. App. D.C. at 184, 383 F. 2d at 706).

That, of course, is precisely this case. As appears more fully in the affidavit of Congressman Eckhardt submitted herewith, the proposed intervenors, all Members of Congress, are at the present time officially and deeply concerned with matters now pending in Congress, whose resolution will vitally affect the public interest. They must have the information which the executive branch seeks to suppress if they are adequately to fulfill their constitutional responsibilities to their constituents. [9]

These facts, of course, clearly differentiate the interest of these intervenors from those of the defendant, The Washington Post.

---

[9] Proposed intervenors believe the above decisions are controlling. See also, as additional support for intervention, *Smuck* v. *Hobson*, 132 U.S. App. D.C. 372, 408 F. 2d 175 (D.C. Cir. 1969); and *Wolpe* v. *Poretsky*, 79 U.S. App. D.C. 141, 144 F. 2d 505 (D.C. Cir. 1944), *cert. denied*, 323 U.S. 777 (1944).

III. INTERVENORS HAVE STANDING TO SUE

Though intervenors believe it is quite clear that the contention of the defendant Washington Post is in fact within the constitutional guarantee of free speech and that, therefore, it is not constitutionally permissible to apply a prior restraint to the exercise of that right, it is not really necessary to determine the merits of the case in deciding that these movants have standing to intervene. Clearly their interests are as much within the zone of interest to be protected by the constitutional guarantees as are the interests of The Washington Post.

The four leading cases establishing the present law of standing are: *Hardin* v. *Kentucky Utilities Company,* 390 U.S. 1 (1968); *Flast* v. *Cohen,* 392 U.S. 83 (1968); *Data Processing Service Organizations* v. *Camp,* 90 S. Ct. 827 (1970); and *Barlow* v. *Collins,* 90 S. Ct. 832 (1970).

Professor Kenneth Culp Davis has pointed out that, as a result of these cases:

"A huge portion of the former foundation of the law of standing was . . . knocked out. The old test of a "recognized legal interest" was specifically rejected. In its place were two new tests. The first, based on Article III, was "injury in fact, economic or otherwise." . . . The second test . . . was "whether the interest sought to be protected by the complainant is arguably within the zone of interest to be protected or regulated by the statute or constitutional guarantee in question." [10]

Even under traditional standards, these intervenors have standing. Their status is even more secure under the new standards. Let us examine them:

There Was "Injury In Fact, Economic or Otherwise"

Congress has been currently dealing with matters related to the power of the Presidency and of Congress with respect to the making of war, the financing of the war effort, and the termination of the Indochina involvement.

[10] *The Liberalized Law of Standing,* Kenneth Culp Davis, 37 U. of Chicago Law Rev. 450, at p. 452.

As we have seen in the Statement of the Case and in the description of the nature of intervenors' justiciable interest, the staunching of the flow of information concerning our international involvement in Indochina constitutes an "injury in fact" sustained by these intervenors in the performance of their proper function.

It is appropriate here to show in a little more detail the interrelation between the content of the Task Force Study and the subject matter of Congressional debate contemporaneous with the Federal Court action restraining publication of some of that content.

While the Justice Department was preparing its case to restrain publication of this highly pertinent material, and while the legal action in the District Court for the Southern District of New York was going on, Congressmen were giving official recognition to the pertinence of the articles by inserting them in the Record. [11]

During the very period during which the temporary restraining order was in effect and was blocking further installments, both the House and Senate were dealing with legislative topics whose subject matter made the content of the Task Force Study germane to the Congressional debate. On June 16, 1971, two votes were taken in the Senate and 4 in the House on topics to which the study is germane.

In the Senate these included the vote on the Chiles Amendment, which barred use of funds supplied under H.R. 6531 (an amendment to the Selective Service Act which provided pay increases for military personnel) to support U.S. forces in Indochina after June 1, 1972, under certain conditions. [12] The vote on this amendment was; Nay, 52; Yea, 44. Thus, a change of 5 votes would have switched

[11] Congressmen McCloskey and Harrington inserted the *New York Times* installments of Sunday, June 13, and Monday, June 14, in the Congressional Record on June 14, 1971 (H–5096–5136; E–5794–5832). On the same day Senator McGovern inserted the same documentation (S–8977–9015). On the next day Senator McGovern inserted the third installment which appeared in the Tuesday, June 15, *New York Times* in the Congressional Record (S–9111–9130), and Congressmen McCloskey and Harrington inserted the same article in the Record (H–5202–5222; E–5878–5896).

[12] Congressional Record, June 16, 1971, S–9275.

[2 2 2]

the result. Also, the Senate considered the McGovern-Hatfield Amendment, also to H.R. 6531, to amend the Selective Service Act. This provided for the shorter cut-off date to December 31, 1971. The vote on this amendment was: Nay, 55; Yea, 42. A seven vote change would have been required to change the result.

It is impossible to say that, had *The New York Times* installment, due to be printed on June 16, been printed that day, it would have changed 5, or 7 Senators' minds; but it is also impossible to say that it would *not* have. It is certain, however, that the articles were of the type that afford the kind of persuasion or conditioning that affects votes on issues like these before the Senate.

The House was on the same day acting on the Military Procurement Authorization Bill (H.R. 8687). The House continued consideration on June 17, 1971, taking up the Nedzi-Whalen Amendment (providing a deadline after which funds under the procurement act should not be used for Indochina war support); the Harrington Amendment (to delete a title of H.R. 8687 providing an authorization for Vietnamese forces and their allies, and local forces in Laos and Thailand); and considering several other amendments variously establishing cutoff dates and restrictions respecting funds which might find their way into support of the Indochina war.

Debate on these amendments was wideranging. For instance, Congressman John F. Flynt, Jr., of Georgia, reviewed what he called the mistaken premise upon which the Tonkin Gulf Resolution was enacted, the misinformation that was afforded the public and the Congress in that connection, the circumstances of its repeal, and the fact that the present war is being waged without a Congressional declaration of war. [13] Congressman Sidney R. Yates of Illinois noted in debate that it is now clear that the facts surrounding the Gulf of Tonkin episode were kept from Congress at the time it voted on that resolution. He noted that we are reading in the press today the results of giving more and more power to the President and deferring to his judgment in the early 1960's [14]

[13] Congressional Record, June 17, 1971, H–5363.
[14] Congressional Record, June 17, 1971, H–5370

Congresswoman Margaret M. Heckler, of Massachusetts, citing the revelations in *The New York Times* of the deceptions practiced on the Congress early in the Vietnam buildup, said it was clear that Congress must now express its will. She went on to mention *The New York Times'* revelation that the Gulf of Tonkin Resolution was drafted three months before the incidents occurred. [15]

Congressman Lionel Van Deerlin after referring to *The New York Times* series of articles, said that he did not think the war would have been allowed to progress the way it has if Congress had been properly informed back in 1964 and 1965. [16] Congresswoman Bella Abzug, of New York, called for full access to the entire McNamara study, saying she believed the information is necessary to enable the Congress to make a realistic assessment of the prospects for a speedy and total termination of the American military role in Indochina. [17]

Congressman Paul McCloskey, of California, [18] Congressman Bertram Podell, of New York, [19] Congressman James Abourezk, of South Dakota, [20] and Congressman William Ryan, of New York, [21] were among Members of Congress who discussed *The New York Times* documents during debate on the Military Procurement Authorization Act of 1971.

The question of candor of public officials during the development and the conduct of the war was a prominent feature of the debate on the Procurement Act, and such question of candor, or lack of it, was related to the desirability of Congressional action or Congressional expression calculated to bring the war to an end.

Nor have the issues which arose in these bills become moot by the defeat of the Hatfield-McGovern Amendment and the passage of the Military Procurement Authorization Act. There are at least four classes of legislation in the House in which the issue will undoubted-

[15] Congressional Record, June 17, 1971, H–5371.
[16] Congressional Record, June 17, 1971, H–5370.
[17] Congressional Record, June 17, 1971, H–5378.
[18] Congressional Record, June 16, 1971, H–5305.
[19] Congressional Record, June 16, 1971, H–5311.
[20] Congressional Record, June 16, 1971, H–5331.
[21] Congressional Record, June 17, 1971, H–5379.

ly be raised again: Foreign Aid Appropriations and Authorization Bills, Military Construction Authorization Bill, Defense Appropriation Bill, and Vietnam Disengagement Act. Also, there is presently a discharge petition on the Speaker's desk for the discharge of the Vietnam Disengagement Act (H.R. 4101).

The interest sought to be protected by intervenors is arguably within the zone of interest to be protected by the constitutional guarantee in question

The 1st Amendment protects and guarantees intervenors' right to access to this information unrestricted by abridgement of freedom of speech or of the press, and this right is clearly within the zone of interest intended to be protected by that amendment. This is clear when it is remembered that Congress is required to deal with subjects including the raising and support of armies, the regulation of the land and naval forces, and the providing for, organizing, arming, governing and disciplining the militia. [22]

These intervenors are within precisely the same zone of interest as that of the professor plaintiffs in the *Mandel* case. Both are within the zone of interest protecting the right of citizens to enjoy the *product* of free speech. Persons who are so deprived because of a prior restraint by government in violation of the First Amendment are among those *intended* to be protected by that amendment just as are those who are silenced by the restraint.

The case of *Office of Communications of United Church of Christ* v. *Federal Communications Commission,* 359 F. 2d 994 (D.C. Cir. 1966) should be noted as one in which the right to *hear* was involved. Certain individuals and organizations sought to intervene in a hearing before the Federal Communications Commission to contest the renewal of a broadcast license. The commission denied intervention, stating that the individuals and groups had no "standing" to appear. Action was then brought under the A.P.A. to review this decision, and the standing of Plaintiffs was challenged. Plaintiff individuals and organizations constituting a listening public were held to have standing. The Court said:

[22] See Section 8 of Article I of the Constitution of the United States.

[225]

"Since the concept of standing is a practical and functional one designed to assure that only those with a genuine and legitimate interest can participate in a proceeding, we can see no reason to exclude those with such an obvious and acute concern as the listening audience." [23]

The courts have been increasingly liberal in holding an interest which is related to the public interest to be one within the zone intended to be protected by the law in question. This is illustrated in the environmental protection cases which have held that the party asserting an essentially public interest has standing. [24]

IV. THE CIRCUMSTANCES OF THE CASE JUSTIFY INTERVENTION AS OF RIGHT

Rule 24(a) of the Federal Rules of Civil Procedure provides that anyone shall be permitted to intervene "as of right" if he "claims an interest relating to the property or transaction which is the subject of the action and he is so situated that the disposition of the action may as a practical matter impair or impede his ability to protect that interest, unless the applicant's interest is adequately represented by existing parties."

As we have seen, these intervenors are claiming an interest relating to the matter which is the subject of this action. As Congressmen, they are so situated that if the fruits or product of free speech is not made available to them, such will as a practical matter impair or impede their ability to effectively perform their tasks as Congressmen. Clearly, a "disposition of the action" by the granting of

---

[23] See also, in addition to the cases cited *supra*, note 3, *Brooks* v. *Auburn University*, 412 F. 2d 1171, 1172 (5th Cir. 1969); *Fortune Society* v. *McGinnis*, 319 F. Supp. 901, 904 (S.D. N.Y. 1970); *United States* v. *B & H. Dist. Corp.*, 319 F. Supp. 1231 (W.D. Wisc. 1970); *ACLU* v. *Radford College*, 315 F. Supp. 893 (W. D. Va. 1970); *Williams* v. *Blount*, 314 F. Supp. 1356 (D. D. C. 1970); and *Smith* v. *University of Tennessee*, 300 E. Supp. 777 (E. D. Tenn. 1969).

[24] *Scenic Hudson Preservation Conference* v. *Federal Power Commission*, 354 F. 2d 608 (2nd Cir. 1965), *cert. den.*, 384 U.S. 941, 16 L. Ed. 2d 540, 86 Sup. Ct. 1462 (1966); *Road Review League, Town of Bedford* v. *Boyd*, 270 F. Supp. 650 (S.D. N.Y. 1967); *Parker* v. *United States*, 307 F. Supp. 685 (D. Col. 1969); *Pennsylvania Environmental Council* v. *Bartlett*, 315 F. Supp. 238 (M. D. Pa. 1970); *Citizens Committee for Hudson Valley* v. *Volpe*, 425 F. 2d 97 (2nd Cir. 1970).

plaintiff's motion for preliminary injunction would result in that impairment.

It may be seen that the provisions of the rule permitting intervention as a matter of right are immediately satisfied when we have shown, as we did in II of this brief, that intervenors have a distinct and justiciable interest, and in III that intervenors have standing to sue. Therefore, we need only show in this section that the facts and authorities cited above fit the language of the intervention rule.

Indeed, many of the cases cited above specifically treat the question of intervention as a matter of right. See, for instance, *Cascade Nat. Gas* v. *El Paso Nat. Gas*, 386 U.S. 129 (1967); *Securities and Exchange Commission* v. *U.S. Realty & Imp. Co.*, 310 U.S. 434 (1940); *Nuesse* v. *Camp*, 128 U.S. App. D.C. 172, 385 F.2d 694 (D.C. Cir. 1967); and the cases cited *supra*, note 9, discussed on pages 7–10 of this brief. See also *Kaufman* v. *Societe Internationale*, 343 U.S. 156 (1952). [25]

There remains for discussion only the qualification in the rule that intervention may not be granted as a matter of right if "the applicant's interest is adequately represented by existing parties." The difference in the interest of intervenors and the added urgency in their case makes it clear that they are not adequately represented by those who might reach accommodation for their respective interests without satisfying the overriding and paramount interest of protecting the flow of information to the public and to public representatives.

For instance, the third item in the prayer for relief in our motion is an item in which The Washington Post either has no interest or an adverse interest to these intervenors.

CONCLUDING STATEMENT

This brief is solely in support of the motion to intervene. If intervention is granted, intervenors will urge that no preliminary injunction should be granted in this case and will support such con-

[25] Although believing that intervention is clearly available as of right, proposed intervenors also qualify for permissive intervention under Rule 24 (b) because their claims and defenses forcefully raise questions of both fact and law common to the main action; and by consenting in advance to limited participation, they insure that intervention will not unduly delay or prejudice the rights of the original parties.

tention upon the basis of the arguments advanced in the Memorandum in Behalf of Amici Curiae American Civil Liberties Union and New York Civil Liberties Union, which was submitted to the United States District Court for the Southern District of New York in *The New York Times* case and to this Court on June 18, 1971.

The proposed intervenors, like the other parties, and this Honorable Court, recognize that a rapid resolution of this case is imperative, and their prayer to be permitted to intervene is made with full understanding of the practical difficulties confronting the Court in the trial of this case in the constricted time frame ordered by the Court of Appeals. Therefore, our request recognizes that the Court could, and should, place such reasonable restrictions on our participation as are appropriate and necessary to expedite the trial of the case. See *Smuck* v. *Hobson*, 132 U.S. App. D.C. 372, 377, 408, F. 2d 175, 180 (D.C. Cir. 1969), and the Committee Note of 1966 to Subdivision (a) of Rule 24. And see, Shapiro, "Some Notes on Intervention Before Courts, Agencies and Arbitrators," 81 Harv. L. Rev. 721 (1968) at 752–756. On their part, counsel will exercise prudent self-restraint in making it possible for this proceeding to be completed by the specified deadline.

It is urged that movants have standing in this case and that they are entitled to intervene as a matter of right. It is respectfully requested that this Court grant intervention as a matter of right or as a matter of equity.

MOTION FOR INTERVENTION

Now come Phillip Burton, John Dow, Bob Eckhardt, Don Edwards, Michael Harrington, Robert Kastenmeier, Edward Koch, Abner Mikva, Benjamin Rosenthal, William F. Ryan, James Abourezk, Bella S. Abzug, William R. Anderson, Herman Badillo, Jonathan B. Bingham, William Clay, Ronald V. Dellums, Sam Gibbons, Ella T. Grasso, Seymour Halpern, Peter Kyros, Parren Mitchell, Bertram L. Podell, Charles B. Rangel, Donald W. Riegle, Jr., James Scheuer, and Lester L. Wolff and ask leave to intervene in this cause pursuant to Rule 24 of the Federal Rules of Civil Procedure in order to assert the defenses set forth in their proposed answer, of which a copy is hereto attached, on the grounds that:

[228]

1. Movants are all Members of Congress and are affected by this litigation. If this litigation prevents the defendant Washington Post from publishing material from the Defense Department's 1968 Task Force Study on Vietnam, they will be denied important information, known to be in existence, which bears strongly on the following extremely important policy questions (among others):

(1) The definition and extent of the authority of Congress and of the Presidency with regard to the war-making power as respects:

(a) the power of Congress to declare war and exercise other authority under Article I, Section 8, of the Constitution; and

(b) the power of the President to act as Commander-in-Chief of the Army and Navy of the United States and to exercise other authority under Article II, Section 2, of the Constitution.

(2) The manner in which the power of the Presidency has been conducted as respects the war-making power;

(3) Whether or not Congress should enact further statutory provisions providing processess designed to prevent the President from overstepping constitutional authority or initiate further statutory or constitutional provisions delineating with greater precision the boundaries between presidential and congressional authority;

(4) The conduct of foreign affairs bearing on the subject;

(5) The matter of governmental organization bearing on the subject; and

(6) All questions relating to the right of the people to secure information necessary to the effective exercise of their function as citizens in a democracy.

2. A prior restraint upon the defendant Washington Post preventing the publishing of material from the Defense Department's 1968 Task Force Study on Vietnam would, and does (as respects the temporary restraining order), constitute prior restraint on the exercise of the right of free speech and freedom of the press as guaranteed by the First and Fourteenth Amendments to the Constitution of the United States.

3. Movants have suffered, and do suffer, injury in fact by virtue of the temporary restraining order as is more fully described in the affidavit of Congressman Eckhardt submitted herewith. H.R. 8687,

the Military Procurement Authorization Bill, is being debated in the House at the time of the preparation of this motion and during the period while the temporary restraining order herein is in effect. The debate upon such bill (as exemplified for instance by that of the Honorable John J. Flynt, Jr. of Georgia, on June 17, 1971) dealt heavily with the policy question set out in items (1) and (2) of paragraph 1 above. Enjoining further publication of matter contained in the Defense Department's 1968 Task Force Study on Vietnam will deny to these movants important facts which constitute their tools for dealing with the important policy questions listed in items (1) through (6) of paragraph 1 above.

4. The interest of these movants is one protected by law in that

(1) Section 8 of Article I of the Constitution places upon them, together with other Members of Congress, duties requiring access to a wide range of information concerning, among other matters, the declaration of war, the raising and support of armies, the regulation of the land and naval forces, the providing for organizing, arming, governing and disciplining the militia, and

(2) The First and Fourteenth Amendments to the Constitution protect and guarantee movants' right to access to information unrestricted by abridgement of the freedom of speech, or of the press.

These and other provisions of the Constitution, and laws passed pursuant to them, were designed, in part, to protect the interests asserted by these movants. Because of the duties placed upon them as described in (1), above, the interests of these movants are distinct and different from those of the members of the public generally. Movants are so situated that the disposition of this action may, as a practical matter, impair or impede their ability to protect their interests, and the representation of their interest by existing parties may be inadequate. Movants' defense also has common questions of law and fact with the main action. Intervention by movants will not unduly delay or prejudice the adjudication of the rights of the original parties. Movants are willing to abide by such restrictions on their participation in this action as this court deems essential to speedy resolution of the issues herein.

Wherefore, these movants pray that

(1) They be permitted to intervene in this cause,

(2) That no further injunction be issued depriving them of information which they would otherwise receive through newspaper coverage were it not for a prior restraint against publication of the said Task Force Study, and

(3) That, whatever decision be made respecting defendant Washington Post, such right, if any, as movants, Congress or any committee thereof have to subpoena or otherwise obtain the documents in question in the possession of the Washington Post or others not be impaired or affected by any order of this Court.

Bob Eckhardt, 3312 N Street, N.W., Washington, D.C. 20007, 202–238–8706.

Thomas Emerson, Yale Law School, New Haven, Connecticut; Bruce J. Ennis, American Civil Liberties Union, 156 Fifth Avenue, New York, New York 10011, 212–924–7800; James H. Heller, American Civil Liberties Union Fund of the National Capital Area, 1424 16th Street, N.W., Washington, D.C., 202–483–3830, Attorneys for Movants.

Congressman Bob Eckhardt, being duly sworn, deposes and says:

I am one of the Congressmen who have moved to intervene in this action, and am personally familiar with the facts which have been alleged in the Motion for Intervention and the brief in support thereof filed by me and by co-counsel. All the provisions of the Motion for Intervention and pages 12 through 15 and lines 1, 2 and 3 on page 16 of the Brief are incorporated in this affidavit.

I solemnly swear that all matter contained in this affidavit, including that incorporated by reference, is true and correct.

ANSWER OF INTERVENORS

Intervenors who have intervened in this action with leave of the Court, answer the complaint herein as follows:

First Defense

The complaint fails to state a claim on which relief can be granted.

Second Defense

The court lacks jurisdiction over the subject matter of this action.

[231]

Third Defense

Plaintiff's claim is barred by the First Amendment to the Constitution of the United States.

Fourth Defense

Plaintiff's claim is an unconstitutional interference with the powers of Congress under Article I of the Constitution of the United States.

Fifth Defense

1. Paragraph 1 of the complaint states a conclusion of law and intervenors are not required to respond thereto. Intervenors deny that any Court of the United States has jurisdiction to enjoin a newspaper from publishing information.

2. Intervenors admit that plaintiff makes the averments that are made in Paragraph 2 of the complaint, but deny them insofar as they are factual averments.

3. Intervenors are without knowledge or information sufficient to form a belief as to the truth of the averments in Paragraph 3 of the complaint.

4. Intervenors are without knowledge or information sufficient to form a belief as to the truth of the averments in Paragraph 4 of the complaint, except that intervenors deny that defendants' actions were without lawful authority.

5. Paragraph 5 of the complaint states a matter of law and intervenors are not required to respond thereto. Executive Order 10501 speaks for itself.

6. Intervenors are without knowledge or information sufficient to form a belief as to the truth of the averments in Paragraphs 6 and 7 of the complaint.

7. Intervenors are without knowledge or information sufficient to form a belief as to the truth of the averments in Paragraph 8 of the complaint, except that intervenors deny that defendants' actions were without lawful authority, and deny that defendants communicated information to persons not entitled to receive such information.

8. Intervenors deny the averments of Paragraph 9 of the complaint.

9. Intervenors deny the allegations of Paragraph 10 of the complaint.

ORDER

On this the—day of—, 1971, came on to be heard the Motion of Phillip Burton, John Dow, Bob Eckhardt, Don Edwards, Michael Harrington, Robert Kastenmeier, Edward Koch, Abner Mikva, Benjamin Rosenthal, William F. Ryan, James Abourezk, Bella S. Abzug, William R. Anderson, Herman Badillo, Jonathan B. Bingham, William Clay, Ronald V. Dellums, Sam Gibbons, Ella T. Grasso, Seymour Halpern, Peter Kyros, Parren Mitchell, Bertram L. Podell, Charles B. Rangel, Donald W. Riegle, Jr., James Scheuer, and Lester L. Wolff, intervenors in the above styled and numbered cause, and it appearing to the Court that the same are entitled to intervene in this cause, it is hereby:

ORDERED, ADJUDGED AND DECREED that the above listed persons are granted leave to intervene in the above styled and numbered cause.

————— —————,

Judge

APPENDIX THREE

Counterbriefing
on U.S. Policy in Indochina

COUNTERBRIEFING ON U.S. POLICY IN INDOCHINA

HON. DONALD M. FRASER

OF MINNESOTA

IN THE HOUSE OF REPRESENTATIVES

Wednesday, February 9, 1972

Mr. FRASER. Mr. Speaker, on Friday, January 28, 1972, a group of House Members sponsored a "Counterbriefing on U.S. Policy and the Indochina War." This effort was cosponsored by the Indochina Education Council, an independently funded resource and research center on the Indochina war located here in Washington. Carl Kukkonen of the education council served as the coordinator.

Our counterbriefing was aimed primarily at the editors and broadcasters brought to Washington to attend a State Department briefing on U.S. foreign policy. We received some attention from Washington and New York newspapers and I include with my remarks newspaper accounts of the meeting.

The participants, in addition to myself, were:

Dr. Raphael Littauer, professor of physics at Cornell University; coordinator of the Cornell research project that produced the report:

Congressional Record, February 14, 1972, pp. E 1169–1177.

[235]

"The Air War in Indochina," which was released in October of 1971.

Fred Branfman, director of Project Air War, a nonprofit educational organization aimed at raising public consciousness about the air war in Indochina.

Senator J. W. FULBRIGHT, Democrat, Arkansas, chairman of the Senate Foreign Relations Committee.

Senator GAYLORD NELSON, Democrat, Wisconsin, sponsor of S. 3084, a bill to provide for a study and investigation to assess the extent of damage done to the environment of South Vietnam, Laos, and Cambodia as the result of the operations of the Armed Forces of the United States.

Earl C. Ravenal, former director, Asian Division, Systems Analysis, Office of the Secretary of Defense; now associate fellow, Institute for Policy Studies.

Profs. Arthur H. Westing, Windham College, Putney, Vt., and Egbert W. Pfeiffer, University of Montana, leading experts on the ecological effects of modern weapons technology as applied in Indochina.

The congressional sponsors were Representatives: JAMES S. ABOUREZK, South Dakota; BELLA ABZUG, New York; HERMAN BADILLO, New York; PHILLIP BURTON, California; JOHN CONYERS, Michigan; RONALD DELLUMS, California; JOHN DOW, New York; ROBERT DRINAN, Massachusetts; BOB ECKHARDT, Texas; DON EDWARDS, California; MICHAEL HARRINGTON, Massachusetts; HENRY HELSTOSKI, New Jersey; ROBERT KASTENMEIER, Wisconsin; EDWARD KOCH, New York; ABNER MIKVA, Illinois; PARREN MITCHELL, Maryland; CHARLES RANGEL, New York; BENJAMIN ROSENTHAL, New York; and WILLIAM RYAN, New York.

Mr. Speaker, under the President's Vietnamization policy, U.S. forces are slowly being withdrawn from Indochina. This is movement in the right direction. But as U.S. manpower levels recede, the air war continues and in some areas it has been accelerated. The nature of the air war means the American public only will be kept informed of this U.S. involvement if the news media make a special effort. That this special effort should be made to describe the air war

[236]

our Government is conducting in Indochina is the point made by all participants in the counterbriefing. A transcript of a tape recording of the counterbriefing follows:

[From the Washington Post, Jan. 29, 1972]
EDITOR'S BRIEFED AND COUNTERBRIEFED
(By Richard L. Lyons)

After hearing administration briefings on Indochina, visiting editors were told by war opponents yesterday that the press bears a difficult responsibility of keeping the spotlight on the continuing but changed war.

Congressmen and outside specialists gave a "counter-briefing" on Capitol Hill for a few dozen of the 400 editors and broadcasters who had come to Washington for a two-day briefing by high administration officials.

The editors were told that the war has not ended, but has shifted from a ground war to a bombing war which reporters cannot see and so cannot report to the public.

Few Americans are now being killed, lessening antiwar pressure at home, but American policy to maintain an anti-Communist government in Saigon remains unchanged the editors were told.

Fred Branfman, director of a private organization trying to mobilize public sentiment against the air war in Indochina, said a third Indochina war is now being waged. The first was by the French until 1954 and the second by American ground troops until recently.

The third, he said, is a war waged from the air by bombers that destroy everything below them. At least half the bombs dropped are designed to kill people, not to destroy structures, Branfman said. He heads a group called Project Air War.

Unlike the ground war, the bombing war cannot be covered by reporters and cameras, Branfman said, and the American people are not getting the facts to form judgments for pressuring Congress to end the war. The war will go on indefinitely, he said, unless the press reports that it is not ending.

Rep. Donald Fraser (D-Minn.) said the recent change in House sentiment toward an antiwar stand was caused by public pressures.

This will be less as ground troops are withdrawn, he said. He called on the press to keep the spotlight on the war.

Sen. J. William Fulbright (D-Ark.), chairman of the Senate Foreign Relations Committee and one of the most outspoken congressional critics of the war, said that if he were President he would do what the French did in 1954 after long, costly fighting—decide it is not in our national interest to continue, and get out.

Fulbright said President Nixon's forthcoming trip to Peking indicates that he wants to end the Cold War. "Why is he so hesitant about getting out of Indochina?" asked Fulbright. He said the President's latest proposals vary little from those rejected by North Vietnam in the past.

Slides were shown of how American bulldozers in South Vietnam have scraped bare an area the size of Rhode Island, how spraying with poisonous herbicides have destroyed forests equal in size to Massachusetts, and how bombers have created 23 million craters 25 feet deep and 40 feet in diameter.

Sen. Gaylord Nelson (D-Wis.) gave these statistics and said he introduced a bill yesterday calling for a presidential report to Congress in six months on the ecological damage done in Southeast Asia by these activities.

The editors were in town for an annual State Department briefing.

TRANSCRIPT OF TAPE RECORDING OF COUNTERBRIEFINGS

KUKKONEN.—This briefing is sponsored by 20 Members of the House of Representatives and was organized by the Indochina Education Council to present information and analyses on Indochina from sources independent and outside the executive branch of government.

Today's meeting is a counter-briefing to the State Department's conference on U.S. policy that was being held for editors and broadcasters. All statements today are on the record.

The war in Indochina has begun its second decade. The fighting has spread to Cambodia and to Laos. The character of the U.S. role in Indochina has changed from a ground war to an air war. Our

briefers today will speak on various aspects of the continuing war and the possibilities for ending it.

We encourage questions from the editors and broadcasters and other people in the audience and in order to facilitate that our format is chosen to promote such an interchange of ideas. Each speaker will give a brief seven-minute presentation followed immediately by 5 minutes of questions from the audience. If we can stick to our schedule we'll be done in an hour and 15 minutes. At that time we will throw the meeting open to a larger group of questions. At present we're missing two of our people; Mr. Ravenal is having plane trouble from Providence, Rhode Island, and Sen. Nelson is on his way.

Our first briefer is Professor Raphael Littauer from Cornell University. He's a professor of physics who coordinated the research project which produced the report on the air war in Indochina. And with that introduction I give you Professor Littauer.

LITTAUER. Thank you, Mr. Chairman.

Ladies and gentlemen, it's rather difficult to summarize such a big subject in such a short time. I'll just try to outline for you a few of our findings.

Air power, of course, is an extremely powerful tool and we know that it's played an important role in Indochina and will continue to play an almost exclusive role in the future or in the near future.

In what ways can air power help to win a war? I think one can break that down into four categories. It can give close support to troops engaged with the enemy on the ground. You have a good example of that, for example, from the Middle East war in 1967 where air power played a decisive role. But you have to have ground forces that are effective that you are trying to support. And of course you are circumscribed by the nature of the terrain and by the type of fighting. And if you look at the Vietnam scene and Indochina scene, you find the terrain is unfavorable as a whole—the jungle. And the style of fighting is flexible and diffuse, again unfavorable to air force which is an indiscriminate type of weapon in that kind of circumstance.

The second role is interdiction of supplies. That is a very important role. Again it is meant to support ground forces, to deprive their opponents of the supplies, and again it is a function of the terrain and of the style of transportation. It is relatively easy to interdict a four-lane highway; much harder to do so against a network of very diffused jungle trails.

Then you have the third category, strategic bombing. This assumes you have strategic targets such as power stations, factories, marshaling yards, airfields. When those targets are few as they were in fact in Indochina, that being a rather rural society rather than heavily industrialized, strategic bombing is limited. You can direct strategic bombing also against the predominant resource of the style of fighting we've encountered in Indochina, which is the population itself. Particularly when it's guerilla warfare the population provides resources, cover, food, shelter, everything you wish to name and is consequently to be regarded as one of the major strategic resources of a guerilla enemy.

Last is deterrence. This is not a direct effect of bombing; it is a psychological or political effect but it does play an important part. I think there is no question that the bombing of North Vietnam in the years 1965 to 1968 had a very strong deterrent motive. It was supposed to teach the opponents that it did not pay to pursue their course. And we will see that deterrence continues to be an important element in the air war as waged by the United States at this time.

Now just to give you a quick thumb nail sketch of the historical survey, I'd like to project a slide (I think we can do that with the lights on) which shows the tonnages by the year which were delivered by air—by the U.S. and its allies but mainly by the United States—to the various theaters of war. And you will see quickly that the main tonnage was of course developed on South Vietnam itself—up to a million tons a year. That is because that was the focus of fighting. On the other hand, that has also been dramatically de-escalated. So when people quote figures on South Vietnam, as

you will see from the other graphs, these are not typical of the air war in Indochina as a whole.

The air war, as a whole, has not come down to half even; it's still more than half of what it was at its great dramatic peak in 1968. North Vietnam stopped as a concerted effort in 1968 as the graph shows there. But immediately after it ceased, the bombing of northern Laos began and you can see from the graph that that was at roughly the same intensity as the amount of bombing removed from North Vietnam due to the bombing halt of 1968. The bombing of north Laos continues. Its effects have been quite extensively documented so I won't go into that.

Bombing of the Ho Chi Minh Trail, which is a specific interdiction function of course, is the major advertised effort of United States air force and as you can see from the graph, it has received increasing emphasis.

Finally we see that Cambodia, since the invasion of 1970, has also participated in receiving a fair share of United States' bombing and that seems to be continuing.

The political impact of such heavy bombing is of course very large. You must not think that the military impact is negligible. It is not. Without it I'm sure the military situation, as it now exists, would not have been achievable without deploying three times as many American troops, general mobilization and so on.

However, concomitant with some military effects, there is a political impact which I think takes a little imagination to understand but it must be indubitably a strong one.

I'd also like to point out that in all this fighting less than 10 percent of the fixed-wing sorties were devoted to close air support. The rest of them, in fact, went to interdiction, to strategic bombing and to deterrence. So that there is a far greater volume of air power shown on that chart than would actually have been needed for the direct military objectives of supporting troops in action. It's important to remember that because air power is a very wide-ranging instrument and the kind of things you do with it of course can be over a wide spectrum of purposes. Thank you for the slide.

Now, for the present trends as we see them is that the direct support function continues to be vital. Reports from both Cambodia and Laos show that without direct American air support the casualties incurred and the defeats taken by both the Laotians and the Cambodian government forces would have been far more severe. Interdiction continues to be very important and of course it is improving. Technological developments, the electronic battlefield, are highly advertised as making interdiction a remote control efficient technological weapon.

However, one should observe that the fighting continues at extreme intensity at the moment and that we have reports of supply build-ups of historic proportions taking place in South Vietnam itself. These reports, I think, indicate that at least the interdiction is not throttling the flow of supplies beyond the point at which the opponents can continue the fight.

Moreover it is difficult to think of interdiction activity as a specific surgical thing you direct against the enemy's lines of supply. When you do that you have to contend with his reactions—anti-aircraft guns, MIG fighters, interference. And the result of that is that your own actions not only drop bombs on the trails themselves but on the airfields, on the anti-aircraft installations and in the general vicinity. The result is that the interdiction activity which by itself seems like a surgical, precise tool becomes diffused through the technology of air power and commits you to doing a lot of things that you're not really intending to do, for example, escalating the war against North Vietnam itself.

I conclude from this that the United States remains deeply involved in the military balance in Indochina despite the theorum that we are withdrawing. And that that involvement carries with it some implications which in the last minute I would quickly like to outline for you.

The policy aims seem to me to be basically unchanged. We have switched, however, to enforcing that policy with a tool, air power, which is basically a mismatch to the objectives it is trying to achieve.

Air power is not a precise match to the requirements of Indo-

[242]

china. We are now relying on it exclusively and the question you have to ask yourself is: In undertaking a commitment to enforce a policy by air power, what will it mean when your bluff is called? That is, when the deterrent effects and when the direct interdiction effects and the close support effects of the air power fail to deter the enemy from his actions, what do you do for encores? That is a question I think that we should all ask ourselves because we are standing on the threshold of such a decision, I believe, in the very next few weeks.

The style of warfare has changed dramatically. We're able to wage that war without bases in South Vietnam. We're able to wage it from Thailand and from carriers afloat in the Gulf of Tonkin. However, the intent is the same; the involvement of U.S. policies is the same: and if we should be pushed, the question we have to ask ourselves (is) how can we respond?

I think the important point is that the cessation of bombing which is not mentioned in many places explicitly is a bargaining token which may contribute to the settlement of the conflict. But it will do so only while it has a meaning. Once it is defeated, once its impotence against the ultimate progress of the other side should become demonstrated it will, of course, be a devalued token and we will have missed the opportunity for playing it.

I think the impression I would like to leave therefore is that it may not be too late to play that token to negotiate on the basis of a full bombing halt all over Indochina, but that opportunity may not present itself indefinitely.

Thank you. . . .

Kukkonen. Our next briefer is Fred Branfman who spent four years in Laos and is presently working as the director of Project Air War here in Washington.

Mr. Branfman.

Branfman. The events of the last few weeks—of the last week in particular—have shown that there's a basic irreconcilable difference between our government's position and the position of the governments of North Vietnam and the other guerrilla forces. That is, the United States is still insisting it has a right to have a say as to who

[243]

is going to rule in Indochina and the other side says it doesn't. Now whether or not one believes that's right—that we do have the right to make that kind of decision—it's worth pointing out that this is what got us involved in the first place 20 years ago. It's what's led to all the fighting for the last 20 years and there's no reason to believe it's not going to lead to an indefinite war.

However, there is a difference, of course. The ground troops have come home. And what I'd like to stress is that we're involved now in a new war, a war we like to call the Third Indochina War, an air war.

What's important here is not simply the tonnages being dropped, whether they've (been) raised, whether they've fallen, other than the fact that it remains at a quite high level—50 thousand tons of bombs a month. What's important here is not whether the tonnages are rising, falling as long as it remains at a high level.

I'd like to stress three basic points about the Third Indochina War. The first is that it's a total war by machine from the air which levels everything below. No matter what kinds of restrictions we try to place on this kind of bombing, when we're bombing in rural theaters like North Vietnam, Laos, Cambodia, South Vietnam we're going to wind up bombing civilian targets; we're going to wind up bombing people's homes; we're going to wind up killing people.

We've interviewed several thousand refugees in Laos—all of whom have lost their homes—and our interviews indicate, almost to a man, that the vast majority of the casualties are civilians and not the military. Of course if we could hit the soldiers the war would have been over 20 years ago. So, first point—total devastation from the air.

The second point is that—and this is really the key—is that bombing is no longer supporting the ground troops. This was the case during the Second Indochina War—our ground intervention in South Vietnam. It has been the case historically. What's new today is that the bombing is the key. We send our bombers out; they level everything; then the ground troops come in—Snoul, Kratie, Cambodia, the Plain of Jars. Asian ground troops come in afterward and

take out the survivors and search for supplies, whatever. They're supplementing the bombing. That's really the key.

And then there's the third factor—the one I want to speak most about because we are talking with the press today and that is, this kind of a war depends largely on secrecy, on news management, on muffling the kind of domestic dissent which ended the Second Indochina War. Most of the bombing in the last two years has gone on in Laos and Cambodia. The Cornell air war study shows that two-thirds of the bombs have fallen in Laos and Cambodia. Actually for the percentage of American sorties it's even higher; I'd estimate anywhere from 80 to 90 percent of the American sorties are falling in Laos, Cambodia and the southern part of North Vietnam.

Now in those arenas newsmen are not allowed out on bombing strikes. There's only one that I know of. One exception to that occurred a few weeks ago when a reporter was allowed to go out at night on a gunship over the Ho Chi Minh Trail. But other than that, thousands of sorties have been flown in these countries and reporters are not allowed to go out on those bombing strikes. It doesn't seem to be for reasons of military security.

Reporters have always been allowed to go out on bombing strikes over South Vietnam. It seems to be an attempt at news management, to keep the war off the TV screens, off the front pages. Reporters are not flown to the scenes of battle in Laos and Cambodia. The kinds of scenes that we had from Khe Sanh back in 1968—reporters flown into Khe Sanh, the war is on the TV screens, on the front pages—no longer exists. Tremendous fighting at Long Cheng—reporters are only brought in on a prepackaged tour for a few hours for the first time in 10 years.

And what we have therefore is that the press can't cover this kind of a scene. We have to ask ourselves, if it was after all the domestic dissent in this country which did a lot to end the Second Indochina War. Suppose the American people could see scenes like this (holds up drawing) on their TV screens or scenes like this (holds up drawing). These are drawings done by refugees who live under the bombing.

By now the American people kind of know what M-16s and mortar shells look like. Suppose they knew that most of the bombs that we were dropping yesterday and today and tomorrow were anti-personnel bombs, bombs which are only meant for people. Suppose they knew that when this kind of pineapple bomb falls, it has 250 steel pellets in it; one sortie—and we're flying 3 or 4 hundred a day—one sortie has a thousand of these bombs. One sortie sends 250 thousand steel pellets which are only meant for human flesh spewing horizontally over an area half a mile long and a quarter of a mile wide.

But suppose they knew that even these were obsolete because they explode horizontally and we figured out by now that the people are hiding in their holes. So we've gone on from that to the guavas, half a million pellets in a single sortie—they explode up in the air, they go down diagonally into the holes where the people are hiding. Suppose they knew that even this wasn't good enough, that we'd gone on from this to flechettes, flechette pellets which are little tiny steel arrows with fins on one end that as they enter the body enlarge the wound and are designed to shred the internal organs.

But suppose they not only knew that but could see it and could see that most of these bombs—whether by design or by accident— were falling on civilians right now. What this does is to raise a very basic issue.

Our democracy is founded on the principle of separation of powers. And, of course, the press plays the key role in this in terms of informing the people about what their government is doing. Now the press can't go out on the bombing raids, can't be under the bombs, they can't go out to the front lines and see the fighting. At the same time the government meanwhile creates its own version of reality with these newSpeak kind of terms, protective reaction strikes against missile sites and all the rest of it. How can the people make any informed decisions about whether or not they want the war to go on? How can Congress act if there's no public pressure about the war? This is the kind of situation we find ourselves in today.

And just to close, I'd like to point out that this has two very im-

portant implications for me. The first is that this kind of war is an automated war, the kind of automated war predicted by George Orwell, when super powers wage war by machine halfway across the globe and their own citizens don't know anything about it and can't do anything about it if they did. It's the kind of war which is lying like a shadow over the Third World, over millions of people in the decade to come. Unless we can somehow solve this problem, unless we can somehow at least let the American people know what's going on so that they can react, I personally feel that an awful lot of people are going to fall under just this kind of war.

But finally there is the most immediate implication. There are hundreds of thousands of Indochinese right now living in caves and holes and tunnels and shelters. Before we wake tomorrow, dozens of these people are going to be burned alive by napalm and riddled by these anti-personnel bombs and cut to pieces by these fragmentation bombs. This thing is going to go on indefinitely until somehow—and I think the press has this key role to play—we can at least begin informing the American people that the war isn't ending and that it's continuing but continuing by air.

QUESTION. Give us the factual background for your knowledge of the use of these weapons.

BRANFMAN. Well, in terms of the weapons themselves, it's simply from interviewing pilots and interviewing refugees. I can perhaps show you a kind of factual basis that perhaps you're looking for.

We'd be happy to show anyone who's interested. We have dozens of photographs—this is a litle girl. If you came a little closer, you could probably see the pellets still in her. When we interviewed, the father held her out and we felt her leg and felt the little steel pellet in it. This was taken in Laos in July of 1970.

These are refugees from the Plain of Jars. There are thousands of them around Vientiane—people from the Plain of Jars. We don't have photographs of the people from southern Laos that we've interviewed. We've interviewed lots of them also.

Every reporter who goes out sees these kinds of things but unfor-

tunately it's just reported once perhaps or perhaps it's not even reported—it's not news.

I might have mentioned there that as the ability of reporters to see things firsthand goes down, the percentage of the news that they report based on official statements goes up, of course. If you can't see the war, you're much more likely to report you have no choice but to report what you see from the briefing and this is how this kind of information is kept from the press. We only got it, as I say, by interviewing the people and by interviewing the pilots who described how these things were meant to work.

QUESTION. Did the gentlemen find pilots cooperative? Do you feel you got an accurate cross-section of the pilots who were operating over there?

BRANFMAN. Well, I went to Danang Air Force Base in November of 1970. I spent about ten days interviewing pilots. I was taken around by the information officer who went from squadron to squadron and interviewed pilots. And then there are other people that I have just met informally. And I think we have a fairly good cross-section. I didn't make any comments about their attitudes. But I don't think there's any question about these kinds of bombs and how they work. I mean it's sort of common knowledge—everyone knows how they work. Everyone knows about the flechette. Here's a photograph of it. This is a North Vietnamese photograph but it's a flechette.

If you go up to CBS, the guy has a flechette right on his bulletin board that he got somewhere. It's no big question. There's no question that these are the kinds of bombs that are dropping now.

QUESTION. Is this the major proportion of the bombs being dropped?

BRANFMAN. This is something I can't prove. Of course, this information is not released by the Air Force. I wish someone would ask the Air Force and I wish they'd tell us just what percentage. All I can say is I've talked to people who are in charge of stockpiling ordnance at Udorn Air Force Base in particular and then just pilots in general and it's my impression that it's at least 50 percent if not higher. This, by the way, stands to reason. After all, we have de-

stroyed most of the structures in Laos and Cambodia a long time ago. It stands to reason that we would go on from that to these kinds of anti-personnel bombs. But I wish the press would find out. I wish the press would demand the answers to these questions. I wish the press would report the fact that when we went to Laos and asked Ambassador Godley to go out on a bombing raid he wouldn't let us. But we could when we were in South Vietnam. I wish they'd report that about Cambodia. Until they do, we can't document this.

KUKKONEN. There will be opportunity for further questions as we get on in the program.

Our next briefer is Senator J. William Fulbright, chairman of the Senate Foreign Relations Committee.

FULBRIGHT. Mr. Chairman, I wasn't quite aware of the format for this meeting. I'm not sure that I'm qualified to brief anyone on the conduct of the war in Vietnam. The basic facts, it seems to me, have been so overwhelmingly discussed and exposed on television time after time that it hadn't occurred to me that that was the matter in question.

Someone a moment ago asked what I would do or asked one of the previous speakers what he would do if he were in the President's position. I might undertake a discussion of this character.

If I were in the President's position I would do about the same as the French. I would attempt to do what the French did in 1954 when they were confronted with a somewhat similar situation. They had been in control of Vietnam for about 75 years and they decided it was against their interests to continue the war. It had been going on for approximately 8 or 9 years. It began about 1946 and this was in the spring of 1954. And it was costing them a great deal.

Of course, we were paying a large part of the costs ourselves.

But even so, the French decided it was against the interests of their country to continue the war so within the course of about 6 weeks they went to Geneva and arrived at a conclusion of the war by agreement which is generally called the Geneva Accords. I think most of you are aware of the provisions of that. If not, you can ask about it later.

[249]

But the pattern is a rather classic one for a situation in which there's a stalemate, neither side being willing or able to win the war in a military way, that is, a decisive victory. We could have if we had chosen to use all of our power but for reasons which previous presidents thought were good and sufficient didn't wish to use. For example, they didn't wish to use nuclear weapons which they could have used and would have certainly demolished all of Vietnam.

To get a perspective of this you do have to, I think, refer to the history of it, the nature of that war that we intervened in. It was a civil war. First it was a colonial war and then later, after the Geneva Accords, I would say it turned into a civil war between factions within Vietnam.

As I was saying, if I were in a position to do anything about the war, I would follow the example of the French. The French were by no means defeated—they had 400,000 plus soldiers there—they could have continued it for a number of years had they thought it was in their interest.

I feel it's not in the interest of this country to continue the war. We can continue it. We can sacrifice all of our domestic affairs and so on if we wish to. It's a question of what is in the interest of this country.

I would follow the example of the French. There are many aspects of that. They had provisions about elections and about withdrawal in two years and so on. Those details, if they're interesting to you, we can discuss.

Neutralization has been discussed. I've advocated that. Many different smaller details. The main thing is a decision to get out, to stop the war because it is against the interests of this country to continue it. It's against our interests because we have no vital interest in being there and because the interest in reforming and revitalizing our own domestic economy comes uppermost in my view. It's because of such things as you've been reading recently—the extent of our deficit, the disillusionment of so many of our people with our government, the general loss of confidence in the capacity of our political system to meet the challenges today.

The urban problem, the ecological or pollution problem, mass

transportation, etc., a great many neglected areas of our national life. I think they are now so critical that this war, which was a mistake in judgment in my opinion, to ever become involved in should be liquidated simply as a balance of what is in the interests of our country; the preservation and improvement of our own economy and our own country. That's all. To me the basic principle is rather simple. You have to make up your mind if that's more important than continuing a base in Southeast Asia for the containment of Communism.

Now some believe that is important. That is traditional, this has been our policy since the beginning of the Truman Doctrine, that there is this ideological contest in being. Well, the President is moving in other areas to try to liquidate, at least ameliorate, this ideological warfare that has been in process since after World War II. And that again, I think, only emphasizes the fact that it is in our interests to liquidate this physical warfare.

These terrible things that you've told us about are extremely embarassing. It's always been, it seems to me, a shameful thing that a country the size of ours should wreak the kind of destruction upon a small backward peasant community which has never done anything to this country because of its ideological obsession. But that's another aspect of it.

There are all kinds on reasons you can bring into it. I simply think we should finish this war and the pattern for doing so is very much like the French.

I regret that the President's recent offer is hardly distinguishable from the former offers made by President Johnson and others. You may find in the fine print a few little differences, but basically it doesn't exhibit a resolution or a determination that we no longer have a vital interest for remaining in control of Southeast Asia or of South Vietnam, if you like; that we're willing to give up our physical presence there and allow those people to determine their own future, with or without the assistance of the North Vietnamese. That would be the basic decision. I do not think that is quite clear in the President's offer. That's why I think it will not be accepted.

Now, are there any questions?

QUESTION. Secretary Rogers told us on the record that for all of the noise Hanoi has made about the President's proposal, it has not been rejected outright. As a result, hope springs eternal.

FULBRIGHT. Well, they have rejected similar ones often before. This offer of $2.5 billion may be tempting to them but I doubt that it is. It's possible that they could for reasons of their own—this has been a long war and it's been hard on them. I've often thought they should have accepted former offers. I thought in the days of the San Antonio formula that they would have been wise to have accepted our offer. I think they've been very foolish, but not as foolish as we have. The trouble is we've got so much involved and it's a big country and I personally feel it's so much more important that this country be made to operate satisfactorily not only for the welfare of my constituents and all of us in this room, but we have been looked to as a kind of example of democracy that can be made to work on a large scale.

It's a great disappointment, not only to us, but to much of the world and especially our best friends, to see us stumble into this very unwise policy threatening really confidence in the very idea of a workable democracy. It's a great blow to all of those who have been dedicated in the world to the principle of self-government and more liberal life for human beings. So it's much more involved than just this one contest in Vietnam. I don't know. Maybe they'll accept it. I wish they would. I'm only trying to deal with what I think of the probability. They have rejected similar ones before.

I think they have an attitude which is hard for us to realize. They live there. They're Vietnamese. They don't accept the assumptions that we make that there are two Vietnams, they've always said that there's one.

We get ourselves in most peculiar positions. We've done the same in China. We have treated them as two Chinas, Taiwan and China, but both Chang Kai-shek and Mao have always insisted there's only one China. It's only a question of which one's the head of it. But we find ourselves in this peculiar position of saying there are two.

Now we say there are two Vietnams. They've never accepted

there are two. The Geneva Accords didn't accept there were two. There was a temporary dividing line.

There are certain assumptions they don't agree with. They think they're quite able to get self-determination themselves. So they look at it differently. When the President says this is a reasonable proposal, well, to our eyes it may be reasonable. I don't think it is to the Vietnamese a reasonable proposal. They think that we're asking them to surrender everything they've been fighting for. I think in time, regardless of what we do, they are going to be independent of us. We can't rely on the colonial system to maintain a colony there indefinitely. It's a question of time.

I'm only saying I'd like for us to recognize the inevitable now and to proceed to revitalize our own country. Now you can call it neo-isolationism if you like. I simply think that America's in such desperate straits that we need to do a lot here at home. The President and his advisers obviously give 90 percent of their attention to this and other foreign affairs. Obviously, no one's paying much attention—no one who matters—to our domestic and local affairs because look at their neglect. So this is the way I come up to that conclusion. It is in our interests to liquidate the war.

QUESTION. Senator, going back to the original question, what you would do were you in the President's position. Specifically, how would you disengage from Vietnam?

FULBRIGHT. Well, that's the best pattern. If you don't want to revive the Geneva conference and it has been suggested they would never be willing to do it because none of them ever had any confidence we were willing to do anything that would likely bring about a solution; if you don't want to find that out, I would make a suggestion or the offer, I would say, in Paris, if you like, that is comparable to the Geneva Accords, that what actually was agreed to at that time by everyone except the United States including China and Russia and the Vietnamese and the French and everyone—I think there were some 10 or 12 countries that signed it except for us. We refused to and you must remember this was at the height of the McCarthy obsession in this country—1954—and Mr. Dulles just

couldn't bring himself to agree to it. He left there and immediately organized the SEATO Treaty and began to try to undo and undermine the decisions of Geneva. And that's a matter of history. But I would make (*a few words here are imperceptible*) which didn't allow the Vietnamese to decide it. They provided elections because at that time the Vietnamese were willing to have elections. I don't think we should insist upon our concept of elections. I'm not particularly interested in how they decide it. And I don't think it makes very much difference as to what happens to it, that is, to the long term.

I have my preferences. I wish that South Vietnam and all of Vietnam would love to have a nice parliamentary system in which everyone treated everyone with great consideration, sort of like Sweden or Denmark or Holland. But if they don't want that, it's their business and it's not, I don't think, our business and we're very presumptuous to think we can go to them, there or anywhere else. We have a lot to do here at home. And I'm not so sure I can with great enthusiasm say to everybody, go do what we do. Have a system like ours.

I like our system. We've got it anyway, I've got no choice. But it is foolish of us to think, to presume, that we should try to translate this system over to a little country in Vietnam or in Africa or Latin America. They've got to work out their own system. That is my basic approach to it and I think it's a matter of detail as to how they will work the details of self-determination. Now I know everyone is repelled. Are you saying that you don't care whether it's Communist or not? Well, I care in the sense of a preference. I do not care in the sense I'm willing to sacrifice the United States for the preference. That's about the way it is. We all have our preferences.

We have Cuba down there. Cuba's Communist. It's much closer than Vietnam. Why do we tolerate Cuba? Why don't we go in and invade them and kick them out and put in our system? Well, of course, that would be foolish to do. I do advocate that we review our policy and stop acting so obnoxious to Cuba. But the State Department doesn't agree with that either.

I would like to liquidate the cold war. It seems to me the President—if there's any significance to going to Moscow or Peking—

leads me to believe and I think the country, too, that he is willing to begin to liquidate the cold war, to begin to try to re-establish normal relations. I favor that. I don't quite understand why he's so hesitant in the case of Vietnam which is the major one. The idea of Vietnamization—that's true these words like protective reaction strikes are very difficult to tie down—seems to me to be an evasion of the real question. Are you or are you not going to liquidate our presence, our physical presence, in Southeast Asia? Do you or do you not think it is in our interest to maintain control of a base there, a base whether it consists of Cam Ranh Bay or all of South Vietnam or only Cambodia or what have you? If he thinks it is, it ought to be very clear and then he could be right. I just don't agree, that's all.

QUESTION. Senator, you're not the President, you're chairman of the Foreign Relations Committee. Is there any new initiative you might institute as chairman of the Foreign Relations Committee?

FULBRIGHT. None that I could think of that would be effective. I've tried everyone I thought of. I've tried persuasion. We've had hearings. I made speeches. So have my colleagues. Senator Nelson's here. He has, too. I don't want to take any more time because he is a very perceptive man and much more persuasive than I am. He usually gets his way in most of the things he tries. But I don't know anything the committee can do. If you've got a good suggestion as to what the committee can do that's designed to bring about a change I'd welcome it. Our country, of course, that's another matter. We're very conscious of the fact that due to various developments, particularly television and its capacity and the development of the National Security Council with a man like Mr. Kissinger, that we have very limited resources with which to influence the course of events. I think the press also is conscious of that sometimes and of their access to the source of the news, too.

Well, thank you very much.

NELSON. I'm not here as a briefer. I just want to thank Congressman Fraser and the others who deferred just long enough for me to take two minutes before I leave because I'm late on my schedule. I

particularly didn't wish to leave without commending Professor Westing and Professor Pfeiffer for the exceptional contribution that they have made in going to Vietnam and collecting the slides and the footage that you will see here today.

The story that their pictures tell describes the war against the land itself with much greater eloquence than any words I or anyone else could summon to describe the situation.

I didn't want to leave either without reminding those of you who do not know that it was Professor Westing and Professor Pfeiffer who went to Vietnam and came back with some very useful studies of the environmental implications of the massive dosages of the landscape by herbicides for purposes of defoliation. These studies, along with the studies that others made too, made it possible for us in the Senate and in the House to have at our command some important facts with which to debate the issue. And I think their efforts made a very substantial contribution towards alerting the public and the Congress as to the problem being created by defoliation. And I think their studies were significant in causing the Department of Defense to terminate the defoliation program.

So those of us who are not only worried about the war and the disaster of it all and the human suffering by all sides, those of us who are also concerned about the environmental implications of this massive medication of the whole country thought that the environmental problems were over with. When you see these films today, you will realize that the military has been carrying on without the knowledge of the Congress or more than a handful, if any. The films demonstrate a massive interference into the environment in a way that no other country has ever done before in the history of warfare because they didn't have the instrumentality to do it.

I made a statement on the floor of the Senate today in which I said that a scorched earth policy has been a tactic of war throughout the history of man; but never before in any warfare has any scorched earth policy as massively intruded, destroyed permanently the soil in the land as we have done here. I think substantial amounts of it are beyond recovery in a hundred years or 500 years or longer. And it's

a disastrous situation which I think if the Congress understood, it wouldn't appropriate the funds to support it. The President, if he could see these pictures and understood the implications, would demand its halt in 30 minutes. The public, if they could identify who was responsible, would throw them out of office. But they'll never identify who's responsible because nobody knows. It is, as somebody suggested here a few moments ago, an automated mechanistic war run from long distances away; in which the people who are making decisions never see the consequences of the decisions they've made and never see the face of the peasant who sees his land permanently destroyed in one 30-second B-52 bombing that destroys all the land he owns and that of all his friends around.

So I just wish to commend the two professors for the remarkable contribution they have made and I would hope that everybody in the Congress could see these films. If 51 percent of either House or both Houses could see the films, that would be the end of this program. If the President could see the films, that would be the end of this program. But nobody knows what has happened there and these films tell the story.

I have introduced legislation today for an environmental study of the nature and character and dimension of the damage done there and I would hope we can get hearings on both sides—in the House and in the Senate. And that we can move to get this evaluation under way.

Thank you very much.

KUKKONEN. Our next briefer is Earl Ravenal, former director of the Asian Division, Systems Analysis, Office of the Secretary of Defense. Mr. Ravenal.

RAVENAL. I'd like to talk for a few moments today about the relation between the Nixon Doctrine and our current overall foreign policies and the situation in Southeast Asia. And particularly about the prospects for a continuation of conflict and confrontation in Asia.

Of course, it's fair to say that this is an inherited war of this administration. But it's also fair to say that this is the same war, the

[257]

same intervention, though it's conducted under a very different set of policies. In fact, this war has been conducted in various guises under a succession of policies from the Truman-Acheson administration to the present day. The rationales have changed and the war remains.

Truman and Acheson commenced military assistance to France and this was even before Korea. This was related, however, primarily to the containment of Soviet Communism in Europe and the desire to help out France.

Eisenhower and Dulles acceded to their various offices. We had the near intervention, a nuclear intervention at Dien Bien Phu. This policy under Eisenhower and Dulles in Indochina was conducted under the rubric of a rollback, a rollback of Communism in Asia, not simply containment. A rollback at least of the expectations of the various parties to the Geneva Convention. And, of course, it was also conducted under an extreme ideological cover.

With the accession of Kennedy and then the Johnson administration, we had an acceleration to a dramatic global confrontation with Communist power. And this became the rationale for the war in Indochina.

The war continued, it escalated, American intervention was intensified. It took different forms. The rationale changed. It became a bi-lateral, global confrontation with Communist power that was conceived to be monolithic throughout the world.

Now under the Nixon administration we have the same war, but we have a new rationale. And it's very important, I think, for us to realize that there has been a very profound change not only in the international system where we have an advent of several strong independent centers of world power. But there's been an equally profound change in the orientation of the United States under this administration towards the international system.

President Nixon and particularly his very academic and erudite adviser Henry Kissinger very clearly perceive the advent of this multipolar distribution of power. The ideology has vanished. They not just in fact acquiesce in this situation and accommodate it, but they're actively cooperating, as we see, in bringing this new interna-

tional system into being. In short, these men in this administration are the architects of the new balance of power in the world. They're very clear about this. They see this in terms of a new global balance of power and they see this in terms of the advent of new regional balances of power—in East Asia, South Asia as we've seen over the last 6 to 8 months, in the Middle East, certainly, and eventually perhaps even in Central Europe.

Now, true to the rules of the balance of power game, one might parody this administration's approach in terms of a parody of President Kennedy's inaugural. This administration will deal with any enemy, subvert any friend, use and play off any government, et cetera, in order to accomplish its purposes. Obviously, this is a sophisticated and delicate and somehow obscure game that's being played.

It might be exhilarating for those few at the pinnacle of government to play the game, but it is incomprehensible to the Congress. It is incomprehensible even to foreign policy experts. And it's certainly incomprehensible to the people. And I would maintain it is an unsafe and unwise policy for this country. And it's ultimately untenable as a foreign policy for a popular democracy because it does not invite nor deserve the support or the participation of the people or for that matter of the press.

Now the question is, under this new policy and this new set of assumptions about the world, what can one expect to see in Southeast Asia. Well, certainly not disengagement. However one once might have interpreted the Nixon Doctrine during its first few years, since Guam in 1969, it is now clear that whatever it might have meant, it does not mean disengagement. At best it means a selective intervention. And it means a new rationale for old involvements under the watchword of stability.

Now stability has always in some sense been a motive of post-World War II foreign policy. In fact, even before that the United States has intervened, has been willing to fight, it seems, in the twentieth century to make the world safe for something.

Safe for democracy under Woodrow Wilson. Under the Caribbean policy of Teddy Roosevelt and his successors, safe for the United Fruit Company or the City Bank of New York. Under Kennedy,

safe for pluralism and free choice. Now under the balance of power dispensation of the Nixon-Kissinger administration, the United States appears to be willing to fight anywhere in the world just for the sake of stability, to preserve a precarious equilibrium.

Now, this is indeed a very conservative principle and yet it is a principle that keeps the United States intimately involved in the vicissitudes of various regions of the world. Now in fact the world is not going to be stable despite the efforts of the United States, despite our intervention, and in particular, East Asia and Southeast Asia and South Asia are not going to be stable. And this will be despite any intervention in force or any tilt that this United States Government wants to administer in favor of one or the other of the various contestants for power in these areas of the world. So what the balance of power philosophy under this administration implies is not stability in the world but a perpetual stablization operation.

Now if we're lucky, and just lucky, this could be brought about by a diplomatic talk or a mere threat of force. But if we're not lucky, it will take the commitment of armed force to create and carry out this stabilization policy.

In the light of this administration's conduct of the balance of power, how should we consider its objectives in Southeast Asia and how should we regard its latest negotiating ploy that was revealed several days ago by the President?

In purely objective terms, even without any particular animus that one might have towards Mr. Nixon, it is unlikely that this administration was really offering anything substantial, that is, anything that would be likely to upset the balance of power in Southeast Asia. If the true motive of this administration, for instance, was to secure the return of our prisoners, then it has engaged in an elaborate evasion of the obvious, the obvious point that is that if the war were ended, it would be perfectly normal to get back our prisoners of war.

In fact, the President is still attaching too many conditions to his negotiating program, conditions such as the stabilization of all of Southeast Asia which is an expansive condition, one that we haven't even heard before, through the mechanism of a cease-fire throughout

that region. Conditions such as the continuing presence of U.S. air and naval power in the region, and certainly conditions such as the election, however fair it might seem in western terms, which would only cause the NLF to surface and expose itself to annihilation. The program, in short, is too little and too late and the negotiating program has the major flaw of not being acceptable to the other side.

Of course, the administration knows this in proposing this current negotiating program. And so one must conclude that the administration is offering this negotiating proposal not so much as an opportunity but perhaps to be read as a threat; a threat that the United States is going to hang in there in Southeast Asia indefinitely in one form or another until the other side agrees on a stabilization of the region or a balance or an equilibrium for this area, Southeast Asia. Therefore, if this policy is not deliberately, that is politically, changed to allow the scope of politics at even force to take its course in Southeast Asia, then we might well see the next three-quarters of a hundred years war in Southeast Asia.

KUKKONEN, I think we have time for about two questions.

QUESTION. I heard you state that you do not expect the proposal sent by the administration to Paris to be accepted on the major flaw that it's not acceptable to the other side.

At the open briefing given by Dr. Kissinger he stated that the only difference of significance between the proposal being sent and the nine-point proposal given us was that we would not withdraw all economic aid, all military aid, all U.S. equipment and all U.S. manpower; in his words, turn over to them and help them defeat the current government. Now do you think that the U.S. ought to include this in their proposal?

RAVENAL. In my own personal opinion, I think that we certainly should include a complete unconditional withdrawal in our proposal. Now the next statement that must be made is that certainly the President and Henry Kissinger extremely exaggerated and misconceived the nature of the Viet Cong and the North Vietnamese proposals. They did not ask us to connive at the overthrow, the active overthrow, of the government of Saigon. They simply have been

[261]

asking us to cease our active support of that government. I think that this ought to be realized. I think that the propagandistic nature of the briefing of Henry Kissinger and the President's address comes through very clearly when one differentiates the substance from some of the rhetoric attached to their presentation of this so-called demand.

But, I would also say that if this is as Kissinger said the only thing that keeps the parties apart at Paris, he certainly is minimizing this because this is not a small matter. In fact, this is the crux of the entire war. This is what the North Vietnamese and the NLF have been fighting for for the last 20, 30 and indeed fighting for since the 1920s when their party was organized, the Indochinese Communist Party. So I think that to say this is the only thing that keeps the parties apart is seriously to understate the issue.

KUKKONEN. We'll have time for more questions after Mr. Fraser and Professors Westing and Pfeiffer.

Our next briefer is Congressman Don Fraser, House Foreign Affairs Committee.

FRASER. I'm going to make my remarks very brief because I think you've heard from people who are far more expert on Vietnam than I. But I would like to touch on one aspect of the debate on the war which I think should be of special concern to the press of the United States.

What I'd like to just comment on is the inter-action between the war and the House of Representatives. Now what has been evident, I think, to observers and reported in the press is that there has been a shift in sentiment in the House of Representatives over the past two or three years. For example, over the past year, the margin of votes needed to turn the House into an anti-war body shifted from something like 140 votes down to 12; that is, in the most recent clear vote on the Mansfield amendment, a shift of 12 votes would have put the House on record in favor of the Mansfield amendment and that occurred last fall. The freshmen Democrats who came into this session of Congress—of them thirty voted for the Mansfield amendment and only 3 against.

The point that I want to make here is that the shift in sentiment in the House has not been due to any internal processes of the House itself.

It was last year when the House Foreign Affairs Committee first held hearings on the Vietnam war, in which critics from the outside with some qualifications were given the opportunity to testify against the war. Floor debates, as any of the press who've watched them know, have not been productive of changes in sentiment.

And if you look at the committee structure, you find that, for example, the House Foreign Affairs Committee has had among its senior members those who have generally supported the administration. This has been the reason there have not been hearings. And when you look at the House Armed Service Committee, which has had the most direct control over the pursestrings for the war in Southeast Asia, and test their basic alignment, you find, for example, using a caucus vote of a year ago which split the Democrats down the middle—about 50/50—that on the Armed Services Committee the Democrats split 5 in favor of fixing a date to end the war and 16 against.

I'm making this point about the lack of effective internal processes in the House to stress the role of the press in carrying on the debate over the war. The fact is that any change, any significant change in the Senate or in the House of Representatives, has been externally generated. It has been generated by the activities of students, by protest marches, by demonstrations, by publicized hearings of the Senate Foreign Relations Committee and all of this reported through the press. This has been abetted by the concern of parents about the drafting of their children to be sent to Vietnam. This point is important in the context of what is now evolving in Southeastern Asia. That is the fact, of course, that there has been and apparently will continue to be a withdrawal of troops so the casualty rates will go down. And this will mean a lessening of expressed concern on the part of families who are worried about their children being drafted and sent there.

But the air war—and this is a point already made—is of a nature that the press will be unable without special effort to continue to

report what in fact is being done on behalf of the people of the United States in the conduct of the war by their government. So I make these observations to stress the special responsibility that I think now falls on the press in the coming months as this war continues and perhaps intensifies in certain respects.

I'd like to finally just comment, give you my own view about the peace negotiations, the so-called secret negotiations in Paris. I think that beyond the admission of failure of the negotiations, that what is suggested by the position of the administration is that there's been no lessening of the ultimate objective of securing South Vietnam in a fashion which will be compatible with or friendly to United States' concerns. This is the history of negotiations in this war.

It seems to me that it might have been possible that this kind of an approach might have worked three or four years ago when we had a half million troops in Vietnam. But the posture of every administration since we became directly involved has always been to place the settlement objectives somewhat in advance of the realities of the situation and thereby precluding the likelihood of settlement. And what seems to me, as one observer now, is that we have lost virtually all of our bargaining power. The air power may represent a small bargaining chip but I think it's very small indeed in view of the history of bombing over these past five years.

My view is that the United States should disengage from the war. My view is that we should take our troops out, close our air bases and desist from any active involvement in the war. I have difficulty today believing that it is in anyone's interest for the United States to negotiate the future of South Vietnam. We lack the power to do so and in fact, I think we lack the wisdom to arrive at a settlement that would have any meaning over the long run.

So I would hope that the administration or perhaps the next administration will reach the conclusion that realism should dictate our policies from this point forward. And realism suggests that we've lost the capacity to substantially influence events in South Vietnam without a prolonged involvement which I think is no longer acceptable to the American people.

KUKKONEN. We have a few moments for questions.

QUESTION. Congressman, both the President and Henry Kissinger suggested during the past week that the United States had already offered the other side a straight withdrawal in exchange for a POW swap on May 31, and that this current proposal that he made public is somehow an improvement over that. Do you accept that we've ever done that, offered them a straight swap?

FRASER. A straight withdrawal to get our prisoners of war back? I'm reasonably convinced that no such offer has ever been made. And neither in public or in private sessions has it ever been intimated that we've made such an offer.

KUKKONEN. Our last briefers have already been introduced by Sen. Nelson and they have some very interesting slides to show you on the environmental impact of the air war in Indochina. I give you together Professor Arthur Westing, Windham College, and Professor Egbert Pfeiffer, University of Montana.

PFEIFFER. I want to say we're very honored at the very kind remarks made about our work by Sen. Nelson and we're very excited about the bill that he introduced this morning. It's the sort of thing we've been hoping would happen for several years now. Like many biologists in this country and throughout the world, Dr. Westing and I have been very concerned about the effects of certain U.S. weapons systems on the environment in Indochina.

Our concern began with our involvement in the herbicide question. As Sen. Nelson pointed out, the program has been ended, having been found to have been very damaging to the Indochina—particularly the Vietnamese—environment. But this doesn't mean that ecocide is stopping in Indochina.

We were last there in August and found that several very devastating weapons systems are still being employed, some even being escalated. And we want now to move right into the slide show and show you what some of these weapons systems are doing to the ecology of Indochina, undermining the natural base of that country, that is, its ability to recover and produce the food and fiber that it did before we went into that area. And Dr. Westing will take over now.

WESTING. Thank you. If we could have the lights we have about 3 dozen slides or so we'll go through rather quickly.

You see before you perhaps a hundred or so craters made by B-52 bombers. Each of those was made by a 500 pound bomb. This is from about 4500 or 4000 feet up. Each of those holes—and there are 23 million of them by our estimate in Southeast Asia—each of those holes is perhaps 30 to 40 feet across and perhaps 20 to 25 feet deep. The amount of land displacement of environmental destruction by the bombing has impressed us enormously.

This is a somewhat closer view of B-52 bomb craters.

Again a view, and here I hope you notice the type of target. This is the harrassing and interdiction fire, 90 percent strategic bombing. The targets are the forests and the fields, the natural resource base of an agrarian, rural subsistence economy.

Here is one B-52 strike. You see in front of you perhaps 700 holes. This was done in 30 seconds. We have this repeated over again five times a day, day in and day out, at least since 1965—1000 sorties a month by official estimates and this is the result: a half a mile wide and three miles long in 30 seconds.

The next picture indicates what that looks like in terms of Washington, D.C. I have to admit I got the idea from Professor Littauer who has such a picture in a publication of his. Starting at the Lincoln Memorial and going as far as the Capitol, you see what a half of mile by 3 miles looks like, having this as one pattern in a pattern bombing by the B-52s. This occurs four or five times over each day.

You see here on the left rice paddies in operation and functioning. On the other side of the river you see abandoned rice paddies that were once a free-fire zone, have now been pacified, but are still not in use. Over and over again we ran across this. Once an area has been bombed, peasants are hesitant to return to their land in order to reclaim it and farm it. There are perhaps 300,000 unexploded bombs just beneath the surface of Indochina. Again, there's a one or two percent unexploded dud rate that the Air Force explains exists. This turns out to be more than a quarter of a million bombs. There isn't a farm family in Southeast Asia that hasn't lost someone

by having the water buffalo or the plow hit such an unexploded dud and then blow up.

Another aspect of the air war. Professor Littauer described it very graphically. These are the side effects. He described the main military reasons for the main military objectives. This is the outwash. Four logs out of five in Vietnam are now riddled with metal and have become useless as timber.

What this picture represents is the now ended herbicide program. These are C-123 aircraft on their way to spraying War Zone C. You see there four planes—there were over 20,000 such flights before the program ended.

This is the result of one such spraying. You see partial damage. This picture was taken a year or two after the spraying. You see perhaps a quarter of the timber trees destroyed and now slowly rotting in place. This is the result of perhaps two sprayings; in an open forest every tree is killed. The area has been taken over by elephant grass, a useless weed which now dominates several millions of acres in South Vietnam.

This is the result of multiple sprayings. This is Tay Ninh Province near the Parrot's Beak. There are over a million acres of South Vietnam that look like this, that have been sprayed multiple times and the result, of course, is that every last tree or essentially every last tree has been killed. This is northern Tay Ninh.

We turn now to something else. This is healthy mangrove, the coastal forests that start at Vung Tau and go on around. We've sprayed about 40 to 50 percent of all the mangrove forests.

Here's a border region between unsprayed and sprayed. The result is utter devastation with no hope of recovery on those 400,000 acres. Of course you also see some of the 500 pound bomb craters.

This is looking at the mangrove forest slightly closer, with the hills of Vung Tau in the background. Four hundred thousand acres will look like this for at least the next quarter of a century.

Still closer. And here you can see in the very foreground that there's been some salvage logging for firewood and charcoal, some-

[267]

thing that frightens us in as much as we have found out through the French National Laboratories just recently that if you burn wood that has been sprayed with Agent Orange the result is perhaps a material called dioxin which is a very potent poison which causes birth defects.

Here is nipa palm commonly used throughout the coastal regions for thatching houses—the walls and the roofs. That's healthy nipa palm.

This is what it looks like after spraying.

This is a picture of a rubber plantation. As a matter of fact, this is not Vietnam; but in Cambodia, this is Mimot in the Fish Hook region. Clandestine spraying operation in 1969 which in a few days wiped out 173,000 acres of rubber and essentially destroyed the Cambodian economy.

This is healthy rubber. That's how it looks as it should.

And here it is—you see in the foreground destroyed rubber trees, again taken over by this elephant grass and in the background the end of the spray area—healthy rubber.

This is just a picture to show you another aspect of the spraying programs. This is in the central highlands and this represents one crop destruction mission using Agent Blue. Using Agent Blue, the arsenical, we have destroyed enough upland rice in the central highlands to feed approximately 800,000 Montagnard their entire diet. This is an intentional crop destruction program which also ended.

This is looking down on that strip from about 4000 feet. You can see the terraced rice fields that were destroyed here.

This is papaya that is just about to die. This is to demonstrate inadvertent food crop destruction. This is a side effect of forest defoliation. It drifted over on to a man's property, onto a peasant's property, and it is destroying his fruit crop.

Again, a similar situation. Drift has caused the death of that jack fruit next to the house and another jack fruit partially off the picture. Jack fruit in this region of Southeast Asia is the favorite fruit. In that particular province 45,000 jack fruit were killed over a period of three days, all of it unintentionally.

This is a picture showing dead poultry. I only show this because over and over again in our peasant interviews we were told by farmers, by peasants, that after a crop spraying or an herbicide spraying that their poultry died. We were never able to track this down in any rigorous way but we heard dozens and dozens of such reports and were given pictures like this.

Another program. Once the herbicide defoliation program was phased out, the bulldozing program was phased in. This is a 45 ton tractor of which there are 150 in Vietnam working seven days a week, 15 hours a day and clearing enormous areas of forestland. In fact, the program started as a roadside clearing program to prevent ambushes.

This is the roadside again filled in with this elephant grass—this was three years ago—from the edge of the road to the forest and it fills in with this useless elephant grass that water buffaloes won't even eat. Once the roadsides were done, we went to area bulldozing.

Here again you can see craters and the last remnants of the Ho Bo Woods. Nine thousand acres were cleared here in a period of 26 days by 30 such bulldozers working en masse. This goes on all of the time.

Here you see an area of about 6000 acres in Northern Tay Ninh from 4000 feet also scraped clean of former forest.

This is a little closer. Again, the B-52 holes and here is a company of bulldozers of that sort that you saw a moment ago going off to work.

This is a little closer. And here you can get a feeling for the D-7 tractor which has a blade 11 feet wide and the size of a crater. That's quite an old crater, by the way. That crater is probably three years old and you can see a little bit has washed in the bottom—two or three feet—and there's a little patch of grass in the middle and that's the extent of three years of natural recovery in one crater.

Here it is on the ground in the Boi Loi woods along what was considered an infiltration route. This area had been pattern bombed, had been herbicide sprayed, and now was being given the coup de grace with bulldozers.

Finally, a few quick pictures on this so-called Commando Vault or super bomb, the 15,000 pound concussion bomb which is used for clearing, for making instant helicopter paths and also as an anti-personnel weapon.

Here it is inside the C-130. You can see the three-foot probe at the front which hits the ground first and insures an explosion about 2 or 3 feet above the ground.

There it is. This is a film clip out of an Air Force film and you can see it is being dropped by parachute and is about to hit.

There it is. It has just detonated. And here's a cloud which will in a moment be 6,000 feet high.

And there's a two acre opening that has resulted in a mature triple canopy forest. Those trees are 150 feet tall. You can see the size of it by seeing the helicopter which is just hovering over the hole. Two assault helicopters can land in one of these moments after the blast.

Here's a closeup. This is one that we flew over west of Danang. This was dropped on to an enemy rocket position.

A little bit closer and I think here it is looking straight down at it from a few thousand feet. And you can also see a few places the conventional bomb crater size.

And almost finally, here is a picture that shows what would happen if it were dropped on the Washington Monument. You would see that people could get killed as far as the White House and of course, anywhere in that inner circle. They could be wounded somewhat further.

And I think this is now the last picture. Professor Pfeiffer took this slide and he wants to say something.

PFEIFFER. I want to first thank Fred Branfman who is with us. He was the one who made this picture possible. He took us to this refugee village. This is the way many people—over a third of the population of Indochina—are now living in refugee camps as a result of the destruction of the countryside which makes it impossible for them to carry out their mainly subsistence farming activities.

You see one of the pineapple bombs that Mr. Branfman has brought with him. This had been converted into a lamp. It was a

dud which they had defused and put to some useful purpose.

We end up with this picture because we think it graphically illus-trates the effect of this ecocide upon the subsistence farming popula-tion of Indochina.

WESTING. I might mention one more thing, a question that was asked Fred Branfman: What is the proportion of this type of bomb to the big crater producing bomb? I tried to get this information through official sources and it's unavailable. However, my informa-tion coincides with Mr. Branfman's that approximately 50 percent of the ordnance dropped is crater-producing and approximately 50 percent by weight is of the anti-personnel type.

PFEIFER. I might say we have a few black and white prints of some of these slides which if any of you gentlemen from the press are interested in them, we'll be happy to give them to you at the conclusion of the program.

KUKKONEN. I think at this point, it's getting along and people are getting tired. But if you wish, we still have a number of us here and Mr. Ravenal is still in the audience so we will be happy to respond to questions for a while. But people can feel free to leave also.

QUESTION. Were the American authorities and the Vietnamese au-thorities aware of your presence there and what you were doing and did they attempt to interfere with what you were doing?

PFEIFFER. We could not have gotten these pictures and this infor-mation without the very good cooperation of the Department of De-fense. We were helped by the Army, Navy and Air Force and Trans-portation, Logistics, Spy Information. They were very cooperative.

WESTING. The embassy was cooperative as well. In fact, for one full week we had the full disposal of Ambassador Bunker's private helicopter.

QUESTION. If a reparations program would be undertaken, is $2.5 billion enough for the recovery of Southeast Asia?

WESTING. I'm sorry, I couldn't answer that question. On the other hand, I would like to again say that this is precisely the ques-tion that Sen. Nelson hopes to be able to answer with that bill he introduced this morning. It has the purpose of looking into just ex-actly that question.

Anatomy of
an Undeclared War

Anatomy of an undeclared war.

DATE DUE			
DEC 15 76			
JUN 29 1977			
MAY 12 1980			
DUE OCT 6 1982			
MAR 6			
MAR 5 1991			
MAY 12 1993			
APR 19 1995			
MAY 9 995			